The Trust Spiral

The Trust Spiral

Why the Media Needs Objectivity

TARA HENLEY

polity

First published in 2026 by Polity Press Ltd.

Polity Press Ltd.
65 Bridge Street
Cambridge CB2 1UR, UK

Polity Press Ltd.
111 River Street
Hoboken, NJ 07030, USA

ISBN-13: 978-1-5095-7093-5

A catalogue record for this book is available from the British Library.

Library of Congress Control Number: 2025950584

Typeset in 11 on 14pt Warnock Pro
by Cheshire Typesetting Ltd, Cuddington, Cheshire
Printed and bound in Great Britain by CPI Group (UK) Ltd, Croydon

The publisher has used its best endeavours to ensure that the URLs for external websites referred to in this book are correct and active at the time of going to press. However, the publisher has no responsibility for the websites and can make no guarantee that a site will remain live or that the content is or will remain appropriate.

Every effort has been made to trace all copyright holders, but if any have been overlooked the publisher will be pleased to include any necessary credits in any subsequent reprint or edition.

For further information on Polity, visit our website:
politybooks.com

Contents

Prologue

A journalist is a person who is willing to destroy his own opinions with facts.

Sebastian Junger (2024), 'When Journalism Dies', National Review.[1]

The day after the 2016 United States presidential election, the team behind New York Public Radio's *On the Media* recorded an editorial meeting that was then broadcast to its weekly listeners.[2] In a raw and unfiltered segment, the hosts, Brooke Gladstone and Bob Garfield, and their executive producer, Katya Rogers, processed feelings of shock and fear and anger, contemplated mistakes they may have made covering Donald Trump's campaign, and pondered how they might cover the new administration. Given that Trump's presidency, according to Garfield, was 'a historic threat to our democracy and to our values', the central dilemma going forward was a tension between straight reporting and commentary. Garfield wondered whether the show should continue moving in the direction of advocacy journalism – 'amp up the skepticism and outrage' and be 'an activist player in anti-Trumpism' – or whether they should pull back as more dispassionate observers.

'Do we try to approach our jobs as leaders of a movement for truth and justice?' Garfield asked. 'Or do we just try to do our jobs as journalists covering journalism and let the rest sort itself out? I'm not sure we can do exactly both at the same time'. To which Gladstone replied: 'I guess I would say I think we can do exactly both at the same time'. It was a stunning moment. A conversation that typically happens behind closed doors was taking place out in the open, allowing the audience to eavesdrop as new editorial standards seemed to take shape.

Those eighteen emotionally charged minutes of radio effectively took an emerging opinion – that Trump was dangerous and that covering him ethically necessitated an abandonment of the news media's characteristic detachment – and placed it squarely within the mainstream. The segment sent ripples out to the furthest reaches of the North American press corps, to journalists who didn't even hear it and likely never would. It helped usher in an activist-oriented era in media, one that wreaked havoc on journalism's credibility and set in motion an accelerating downward spiral of trust that continues to this day. According to 2025 Gallup polling,[3] just 28 per cent of Americans reported a 'great deal' or 'fair amount' of trust in mass media to report the news 'fully, accurately and fairly' – with a mere 8 per cent of Republicans reporting a great deal or fair amount of trust. While confidence in media has been declining since the 1970s, Gallup registered a significant drop in 2016, and it is now at a record low. In fact, the decline in trust in the media is 'sharper and deeper' than in any other American institution.[4]

Industry leaders have offered various reasons for this decline, attributing it to everything from the rise of social media and misinformation to bad actors online and hostility from politicians, including Trump's barbs that the media is 'the enemy of the people' and 'fake news'. While such factors no doubt contribute, these explanations lack self-reflection and are out of step with the feedback that we rank-and-file journalists regularly hear from the public. If the media wants to restore public trust, we have to examine our own actions. Unpacking our role is essential for making sense of the crisis in media, and for forging a sustainable path forward for North America's fourth estate. To understand the downward trust spiral, then, we must begin by looking at its origins in the first Trump era, and in the fear that drove it.

1

An Existential Crisis

Leading up to the 2016 election, the US media collectively lost its cool. Trump had long been a source of entertainment, a smug punchline, a ratings boon. But as election day neared, his habit of disparaging the press began to grate, and his knack for dominating the news cycle with outlandish claims started to raise legitimate alarms. The feeling that Trump was an extraordinary candidate, and that ordinary journalism was insufficient to the task of covering him, began to solidify.

David Mindich, a journalism professor at Saint Michael's College in Vermont at the time, detailed this shift in the *Columbia Journalism Review*,[1] noting in July of 2016 a change in tone among the likes of Megyn Kelly, Anderson Cooper, and Jake Tapper, who had all become more openly confrontational. Mindich characterized the conundrum facing the press as a 'Murrow moment', in reference to Edward R. Murrow, the CBS newsman who famously set aside his own detachment to speak out against Joseph R. McCarthy in 1954: 'If a politician's rhetoric is dangerous, Murrow implied, all of us, including journalists, are complicit if we don't stand up and oppose it.'

That same month, New York University journalism professor Jay Rosen published a piece in the *Washington Post*[2] making the case that Trump was 'crashing the system' and that the press should pivot. 'Trump isn't behaving like a normal candidate; he's acting like an unbound one', Rosen reasoned. In response, journalists should 'do things they have never done', things that may even 'shock us'. Trump was 'a special case', he stressed, and 'the normal rules do not apply'.

Writing in the *New York Times* the following month, Jim Rutenberg was even more explicit.[3] 'If you're a working journalist and you believe that Donald J. Trump is a demagogue playing to the nation's worst racist and nationalistic tendencies, that he cozies up to anti-American dictators and that he would be dangerous with control of the United States nuclear codes, how the heck are you supposed to cover him?' Rutenberg asked. 'Because if you believe all of those things, you have to throw out the textbook American journalism has been using for the better part of the past half-century, if not longer, and approach it in a way you've never approached anything in your career.' That would be a move, he conceded, into 'uncharted territory for every mainstream, nonopinion journalist I've ever known, and by normal standards, untenable'.

By the time the election arrived in November, the verdict was in: these were not normal times. And extreme threats called for extreme measures. *Washington Post* media columnist Margaret Sullivan penned a column in the hours after Trump won, 'A call to action for journalists covering President Trump',[4] capturing the prevailing mood. In it, she was unequivocal: 'We have to be willing to fight back.' And indeed, this rallying cry was eventually taken up by journalists across the continent. 'It's been an education for all of us, a gradual realization that the instincts and conventions of traditional journalism weren't good enough for this moment in our country's history', Sullivan later reflected in an adapted excerpt from her memoir, *Newsroom Confidential: Lessons (and Worries) from an Ink-Stained Life*.[5] 'When covering politicians who are essentially running against democracy, old-style journalism will no longer suffice.'

Like Sullivan, many in the press were terrified by what they viewed as creeping fascism. But some attempted to turn down the temperature on the discourse. The legendary *Washington Post* editor Marty Baron, for instance, warned at an industry conference, 'We're not at war with the administration, we're at work.'[6] In a widely shared memo,[7] *Reuters*'s then editor-in-chief Steve Adler reminded staff that the service reported from more than 100 countries, including authoritarian nations where visa denials, censorship, and physical and legal threats were not uncommon. *Reuters* responded to all of this, he said, by 'recommitting ourselves to reporting fairly and honestly, by doggedly gathering hard-to-get information – and by remaining impartial'. Adler cautioned reporters not to make the story about themselves, to focus on serving the public interest, and to resist taking 'too dark a view of the reporting environment'.

The press panicked anyway and pulled down its guardrails, a move that many argued was justified by the exceptional circumstances.

Guardrails exist for a reason, though, and discarding them came with unintended consequences. Consider 'false balance', the critique that journalists, in their quest to be fair, often erroneously present two sides of a debate as equally valid. The *Times*'s public editor Liz Spayd wrote in September of 2016[8] that the term was frequently used to attack outlets for reporting on Hillary Clinton's failings, under the logic that Donald Trump's were far worse. 'The problem with false balance doctrine is that it masquerades as rational thinking', Spayd argued. 'What the critics really want is for journalists to apply their own moral and ideological judgements to the candidates.' To illustrate the pitfalls of this line of thinking, she referenced a segment on Brian Stelter's *Reliable Sources*. During the CNN show's discussion of false balance, *Slate*'s Jacob Weisberg said that the press was accustomed to covering candidates that were apples and oranges. But now, Weisberg told Stelter, they were covering an election in which one candidate was a fruit and the other was rotten meat. To Spayd that sounded like 'a partisan's explanation passed off as a factual judgment'. She pointed out that both Trump and Clinton were uniquely distrusted and disliked, with 'the lowest approval ratings in history', and maintained that there was no reason why both shouldn't be scrutinized: 'If ever there was a time to shine light in all directions, this is it.' Tearing down a guardrail that aims to ensure balance, she warned, could ultimately result in power not being held to account – 'all power, not just certain individuals'.

Consider, too, the newsroom taboo against labelling a politician's statement a 'lie', since the word is inflammatory and denotes not only an untruth but an intent to deceive, which is hard to prove. Ahead of the 2016 election, the *Times* opted to use that word in a front-page headline about Trump. While Spayd agreed that it was warranted in select cases, she cautioned colleagues that it should be used sparingly: 'Its power in political warfare has so freighted the word that its mere appearance on news pages, however factually accurate, feels partisan.'[9] Indeed, many had reservations about using 'lie' at all. As the investigative reporter Matt Taibbi said in a CBC documentary that aired in 2021, 'Once you take that step into becoming kind of a political actor instead of a journalist, the problem is you can't go back.'[10]

That is exactly what happened. The erosion of journalistic norms and practices did not remain limited to Trump coverage or even to the Trump era. Instead, new emergencies continually emerged: Russian interference in American politics, #MeToo, the pandemic, the racial reckoning, and so on. The exception became the rule. 'The media in the last four years has devolved into a succession of moral manias', Taibbi wrote in 2020.[11] 'We are told the Most Important Thing Ever is happening for days or weeks at a time, until subjects are abruptly dropped and forgotten, but the tone of warlike emergency remains.' With each new cause for alarm and each new reason to take a strong stand, the media has been pushed further down the slippery slope of activism. 'We're living in times where everything is overblown and dire and an emergency', David Greenberg, a professor of history and journalism at Rutgers University, told me in 2022.[12] 'In that context, there's a sense of desperation – that we need to assert moral truths, unambiguously.'

Such an imperative inevitably leaves us open to 'ideological capture', when an ideology assumes disproportionate influence over, in this case, a newsroom and its operations. It stifles critical thinking and paves the way for factual errors, which engender hostility among the public. In the face of that mounting anger, we double down on certainty, refusing to admit mistakes lest we cede ground to actors or ideas that we consider malevolent, thereby further eroding norms and practices. Such behaviour leaves the citizens we are meant to serve ever more distrustful of our work. And with each new downward cycle, they abandon us in ever greater numbers. Our credibility, our morale, and our ability – both emotionally and financially – to evaluate the facts is diminished, which makes us more desperate, more anxious.

This anxiety of ours, it must be said, predates Trump. Indeed, the unravelling of trust in the media would not have been possible if our business had not already been on the edge of a precipice when he got into politics – if individual journalists' lives and the state of entire media organizations was not already so precarious.

So the first stage of the trust spiral is not political at all but economic.

2

A Failing Business Model

There's an old saying about how you go broke, the Canadian journalist and commentator Jen Gerson told me recently: 'Slowly, slowly, and then all at once.'[1] This is the case for the news media, she said, which has slowly been going broke for the past two decades and is now all collapsing simultaneously. The business on both sides of the border has been grappling with catastrophic declines in revenue, mass lay-offs, and outlet closures for years. And now the bill is finally coming due.

A single month in early 2024 offered ample evidence. 'For a few hours last Tuesday, the entire news business seemed to be collapsing all at once', Paul Farhi wrote in *The Atlantic* in January,[2] lamenting lay-offs at *Time*, *National Geographic*, and the *Los Angeles Times*. Sewell Chan, then editor-in-chief of the *Texas Tribune*, a non-profit site, told Farhi that he worried that 2023–4 could see an 'extinction-level event' not unlike the 2008 recession. These downsizings were followed by cuts at *Business Insider* and the folding of the well-funded start-up *The Messenger*. The shuttering of *Vice.com* came next. Then, in early 2025, came lay-offs at NBC, *HuffPost*, *Vox Media*, and CNN. Close to 10,000 journalists were laid off in three years, noted Katherine Reynolds Lewis, founder of the Institute for Independent Journalists, in a piece for *Nieman Reports*,[3] drawing on Bureau of Labor Statistics data. This amounted to more than one in ten of the reporters and editors in the entire industry. As she put it, 'layoffs are the new normal'.

But for much of the twentieth century, the news media enjoyed well-staffed newsrooms, large readerships, viewers, and audiences, and robust advertising revenues – until the advertising business model began to implode with the rise of the internet. First, Craigslist rendered the classified sections of newspapers obsolete, decimating a reliable and crucial moneymaker. Next, particularly in the aftermath of the 2008 recession, outlets lost commercial ad revenue. And as tech giants like Facebook and Google broke new ground on digital advertising, offering targeted ads with detailed analytics, even more dollars went out the door. 'I think people have underestimated the size of this disruption', Peter Menzies, a former newspaper executive and former vice-chair of the Canadian regulatory body the Canadian Radio-television and Telecommunications Commission (and later my co-host on the Full Press podcast), told me of the digital revolution.[4] 'It's analogous to the invention of the printing press.'

As this massive shift unfolded, the range of content available online exploded, attention spans fragmented, and the public began turning away from television news. As Taibbi has detailed in his book *Hate Inc.: Why Today's Media Makes Us Despise One Another*,[5] to compete for elusive eyeballs, TV executives targeted specialized demographics. Fox News, founded in 1996, rose to prominence in the 2000s by going after conservatives, and MSNBC used the same formula to court liberals. The combined effect was a media ecosphere with more opinion, more outrage, more division. 'We have today a very polarized media environment', Batya Ungar-Sargon, a former opinion editor at *Newsweek*, told me in 2022.[6] 'But it's polarized only on behalf of . . . rich liberals and rich conservatives.' For the vast majority of Americans, she continued, 'the media is just not talking to them, or about them, or about anything they care about. They're completely checked out, and they're increasingly boycotting the mainstream media.'

The business model for news used to be based on attracting as large an audience as possible. But as that model collapsed – and as an engagement-driven model emerged – digital outlets were incentivized to cultivate niche audiences. Since the most extreme audiences were also the most engaged, this new business model rewarded content that appealed to ever narrower demographics. Then, as the engagement model itself began to fail, a small group of marquee outlets successfully transitioned to subscriber models by cultivating urban, educated audiences that were willing and able to pay, including the 12.33 million who now subscribe to the *New York Times*. Most others floundered. Jobs were slashed and operations were consolidated. Local news, meanwhile, increasingly disappeared. (According to the Local News Initiative at Northwestern University, more than 3,200 print newspapers closed between 2005 and 2024, with fewer than 5,600 remaining, most of them weeklies.[7] In 2024, *Axios* noted that more than half of American counties had either a single local news source or none whatsoever.[8] Though it made huge advances, enjoying the benefits of technological innovation in accessing data, and requiring considerably less manpower than previous eras, investigative reporting – the most expensive and time-consuming form of journalism – suffered for lack of overall resources, as well. The newsrooms left standing were significantly weakened, as was the quality of their coverage.

Predators also moved in. Hedge funds bought up newspapers, sold off real estate, and extracted as much money as possible from outlets. They laid off staff, leaving skeleton teams in place. 'Papers eventually are driven into the ground', Sohrab Ahmari, the author of *Tyranny, Inc.: How Private Power Crushed American Liberty – and What to Do About It*, told me.[9] 'But more often, private equity holds on to them as ghost papers. Ghost papers typically do a lot of vacuous, advertorial-type content. Then, in between, they run mostly national coverage. Because national coverage is easy to syndicate across many papers.' The problem is the loss of 'the local media watchdog function, and that element of local media as being crucial to the local democratic conversation'. If a paper shuts down entirely, the community pays what amounts to a 'corruption tax', to repeat a phrase used by former *Boston Globe* editor Ellen Clegg, the co-author with journalism professor Dan Kennedy of *What Works in Community News: Media Startups, News Deserts, and the Future of the Fourth Estate*.[10] 'There's no watchdog watching the local budget', she told me.[11]

Jen Gerson, who used to work at the *Calgary Herald* newspaper in Canada, prefers the term 'zombies'. By the time she left that paper, she was writing straight to the page, without her copy being checked by editors. 'Typos went up, errors went up', she told me on my podcast, *Lean Out*, in 2023.[12] 'As the editing process collapsed in on itself, the institutional judgement and norms that had been established from the previous century of journalism, that came under threat.' Prior to the Trump era, 'a lot of these things are already on really shaky ground'.

In such a climate, the training of young journalists naturally deteriorated. And that is key to understanding the mess we are in. As Bill Kovach and Tom Rosenstiel noted in their classic text, *The Elements of Journalism: What Newspeople Should Know and the Public Should Expect*,[13] in past decades as journalism professionalized, 'the press organized itself into chains' and 'companies began to use their newspapers and TV stations as farm systems to train journalists in small markets for later assignments in bigger ones'. The downside of this, the authors pointed out, was parachuting transient journalists into communities they were unfamiliar with and felt less invested in.

But the upside was exposing journalists to a broad range of locales and perspectives and providing extensive on-the-ground training, with opportunities to learn and make mistakes in lower-stakes settings. Journalism is not something that you can learn at university, the publisher of the Ottawa-based outlet *Blacklock's Reporter*, Holly Doan, told me.[14] You have to apprentice. And the disappearance of smaller outlets has meant fewer opportunities to do just that: train for years at local publications, and then regional ones, living in communities across the country before finally arriving in the capital to cover national stories. 'That doesn't happen anymore. Now you have journalists who go to journalism school, where they're not taught anything about covering courts or local council', she said. 'The skills are gone. Journalism isn't dying. On the ground level, it's dead.'

A generational shift in skills has been compounded by a generational shift in class background. According to *The 2022 American Journalist Study*, a research project supported by the S.I. Newhouse School of Communications at Syracuse University that builds on some five decades of data, 96.4 per cent of full-time journalists in the US now have a college degree, up from 58.2 per cent in 1971.[15] Newsrooms today are staffed almost exclusively by college grads, often with degrees from tony academic institutions. Indeed, Nieman Journalism Lab founder Joshua Benton found that about 27 per cent of the *New York Times* journalists that listed their schooling online held Ivy League degrees.[16] A study from the University of Arkansas's Jonathan Wai and Kaja Perina examined 1,979 employees of the *New York Times* and the *Wall Street Journal*; about half had attended one of twenty-nine top colleges.[17] Prestige schooling and competition-induced credentialism, coupled with the requirement to undergo unpaid or poorly paid internships in expensive cities, favours young people from economically privileged families. This trend has reduced the economic diversity of newsrooms, and reinforced the perception that the media belong to society's elites, despite the industry's dismal financial prospects.

The media has not just become concentrated in certain economic classes, though. Corporate consolidation has also produced high levels of geographic concentration, with many journalists based in a handful of major urban centres, cut off from the range of perspectives elsewhere. In 2019, Pew Research found that more than one in five American newsroom employees lived in New York, Los Angeles, or Washington, D.C.[18] (This data was collected before the pandemic's remote work policies, however, which may have made a dent in the overall trend). Steve Krakauer, the executive producer of *The Megyn Kelly Show*, highlighted such geographic bias in his book, *Uncovered: How the Media Got Cozy with Power, Abandoned Its Principles, and Lost the People*,[19] referring to the modern press corps as the 'Acela media', after the Acela train that runs between Washington and Boston.

This geographic bias helps explain some of the missteps of the Trump era, he told me. It was, he said, something that he only fully comprehended when he moved from New York to Texas. 'The fact is that when Donald Trump was elected in November of 2016, it was such a shock to the system', Krakauer said.[20] 'There was this existential threat that they were fighting against to save democracy . . . Most of the people that I encounter here in Dallas, Texas, who are not overly political – maybe lean left, maybe lean right – they are not thinking about the world during those years in the same way the media did.'

The journalist Andy Mills, formerly of the *New York Times*, also drew attention to this blind spot in a recent conversation.[21] He told me that reporting from the Midwest, a lot of the communities he encounters are shells of their former selves. 'It is a desolate scene in many of these places', he said. 'I'm talking ghost towns. Not just empty factories, but because of that, abandoned homes.' People in these places felt that the country was no longer serving them, and that the media was telling them what to believe instead of reporting their experiences.

But the unfolding disruption of the internet era, and its erosion of legacy media, did not just result in economic and geographic concentration – it also incentivized ideological bias.

The digital publications that initially found success during the aughts and 2010s, largely funded by private capital, were often more openly partisan than traditional media. That was the case with first *The Drudge Report* on the right and then *The Huffington Post* (now *HuffPost*) on the left. Many digital pioneers, and those who emulated them, prioritized virality over truth-seeking, giving rise to an era of gossip blogs, personal essays, listicles, and off-the-cuff opinion pieces driven by outrage (with headlines like 'This brave woman's horrifying photo has become a viral rallying cry against sexual harassment'[22] and 'The problematic Disney body image trend we're not talking about'[23]).

This ascendant 'anti-media', as the writer Vanessa Grigoriadis memorably put it in *New York Magazine* in 2007, was remarkably anti-establishment.[24] It was, she wrote, fuelled by 'the anxiety and class rage of New York's creative under-class'. For them, a $200,000-a-year job, 'once an attainable goal for those who had climbed near the top of the ladder in editorial departments, has all but disappeared' – not to mention the ability to buy a home anywhere even remotely near their offices. The contemptuous New York media gossip blog Gawker, in particular, Grigoriadis wrote, existed as 'a catalogue of the decline of New York print publishing, an entire history of the fall'. Its 'social-policing and snipe-trading sideshow' was 'a kind of moral drama about who deserves success and who doesn't . . . a Manhattan version of social justice'. All of this occurred before the Great Recession even hit, with the subsequent decade seeing the elimination of one in four newsroom jobs.[25]

The anarchic, snark-driven genre that was the hallmark of these blogs required little expertise – and zero reporting – to produce. And its explosive virality led to the rise of content farms. One notable example, PolicyMic, the precursor to Mic, apparently published between fifty and 100 stories a day, written by 2,500 freelancers and edited by just twenty staff.[26] Meanwhile, as Grigoriadis reported, many of Gawker's writers were paid to pen a dozen posts a day (at $12 a post), with their editors expected to edit a piece every fifteen minutes. One of the site's stars, Emily Gould, described her job as 'a weird cross between being an artist and working in a sweatshop'.

The more desperate the failing legacy outlets became, the more they chased traffic, recruiting the poorly paid digital natives employed by these high-volume outlets, assuming they could reliably attract eyeballs. And these young journalists were increasingly influenced by a niche political culture that was popularized on early sites like Jezebel, took hold on places like Tumblr, and gained enormous traction on social media.

It was this new ideology that truly accelerated the media's trust spiral.

3

A Great Awokening

In his book *Canceling Comedians While the World Burns*,[1] the *Jacobin* columnist Ben Burgis describes a YouTube clip from a 2019 Democratic Socialists of America convention, which he briefly attended. In it, the gathering is repeatedly disrupted by delegates who complain about fellow participants standing (too distracting), whispering (too triggering), and wearing cologne and perfumes (too aggressive). They ask that delegates avoid clapping (jazz hands work just fine) and gendered language like 'guys'.

The video, which of course cherry-picks moments from many hours of a live-streamed event, was gleefully mocked on conservative media platforms. Still, Burgis, who'd been a DSA delegate in the past, told me, 'Nothing that I saw in there surprised me in the least.'[2] It was, he said, unfortunately 'very familiar behaviour, this kind of scolding one-upmanship'. What bothered him most about the clips, he said, was that everybody knew the conference was being broadcast, underscoring a troubling gap between activist subculture and mainstream public opinion. 'I think that once you're inside that bubble', Burgis said, 'it can be easy to forget how that reads to everybody else outside of it'. The clips highlighted, albeit in a comically exaggerated way, a belief system that took over not just progressive politics but many of North America's most influential institutions, from the arts to education.

This set of beliefs proved remarkably resistant to critical evaluation, for several reasons. First, because it branded itself as a social justice movement, and few people see themselves as being against a just society. Second, because it presented its ideas as moral imperatives – as basic human decency – and few want to be considered immoral. Third, because its adherents contested attempts to name their movement, arguing that the term 'woke' is a slur and that those who used it were not able to define it, which obviously made the movement harder to discuss. And fourth, because its more extreme members shut down debate entirely, with vicious campaigns of online shaming. 'What we have actually seen develop in the States', the podcaster and media entrepreneur Kmele Foster told me for a 2021 *Globe and Mail* newspaper feature, 'is a real appetite right now to punish people who have bad ideas. And the universe of things that are considered bad, objectionable ideas is expanding at a pretty rapid clip.'[3] But as the podcaster and commentator Chloé Valdary said in a separate conversation for that same piece, 'Complexity of ideas, and the ability to hear from people who we disagree with, is critical for a functioning democracy.'

The exercise of critiquing this movement is made no less perilous by the fact that its most famous opponent has been Donald Trump, and many will be loath to be associated in any way with his agenda. Nonetheless, those who want to understand declining trust in media must understand the role that this ideology has played. So, unpacking it remains a vital task, despite its many minefields. We can start by using as neutral a term as possible: 'identitarian moralism'. And by attempting as neutral a definition as possible: a political philosophy that examines social inequalities through the lens of identity and considers it a moral obligation to dismantle group disparities.

Having established what is, in fact, a definable political ideology, we should then feel free to evaluate it critically, as we would with any other. In doing so, we might notice that while identitarian moralism is radical on social issues like race and gender, it does little to challenge the economic status quo, which may be why it was initially embraced by so many corporations. We might also notice that while it presents itself as leftism, it dispenses with key tenets of the left, from universalism to free speech, and largely ignores material conditions and class analysis. In many ways, identitarian moralism actually disdains the working class, whose members fail to conform to its ever-shifting mores. These mores have included transforming language and speech norms; interrogating interpersonal relationships; problematizing pop culture; increasing the representation of marginalized groups in elite spaces; enforcing symbolic gestures such as land acknowledgements; enacting diversity, equity, and inclusion training sessions; and building up an identity-focused bureaucracy to advance such efforts.

Identitarian moralism, it must be said, has been particularly popular among media workers, as the Marxist writer Freddie deBoer pointed out in a scathing essay in 2021.[4] 'In the span of a decade or so, essentially all professional media not explicitly branded as conservative have been taken over by a school of politics that emerged from humanities departments at elite universities and began colonizing the college educated through social media', he wrote on Substack. 'Those politics are obscure, they are confusing, they are socially and culturally extreme, they are expressed in bizarre vocabulary, they are deeply alienating to many, and they are very unpopular by any definition.'

DeBoer asked, 'Why does no one in media seem willing to have an honest, uncomfortable conversation about the near-total takeover of their industry by a fringe ideology?' (It was as if, he told me later, 'the whole media crawled into a very narrow hole'.[5]) The author of *How Elites Ate the Social Justice Movement*,[6] deBoer is not the only leftist thinker to blast this brand of progressive politics. The Berlin-based philosopher Susan Neiman has published an influential critique, *Left Is Not Woke*,[7] based on the Tanner Lecture that she delivered at the University of Cambridge. The Marxist scholar Adolph Reed Jr has written extensively on the topic as well. So too have others across the political spectrum, including John McWhorter, Coleman Hughes, Yascha Mounk, Noah Rothman, Andrew Doyle, Eric Kaufmann, and Irshad Manji, and many have highlighted its prevalence in the mainstream media.

Even so, journalists often reject the claim that coverage has been overly influenced by this ideology. And to be fair, its influence can be difficult to quantify. Much of the conversation around 'woke' bias relies on critiques from partisan actors, selectively chosen articles, anecdotal evidence from frustrated media workers, and online complaints from the public, which, while certainly plentiful, may not be fully representative of public opinion. Such evidence can be easy to dismiss. And although Pew Research did find in 2020 that nine out of ten people who listed the *New York Times* as their main news source identified as Democrats[8] – suggesting that the paper is very friendly to the Democratic Party – statistics on audience partisanship tend to be difficult to obtain. Still, the fact that in recent years such indicators have generally pointed in the same direction should at least give us pause.

That is especially true alongside a more compelling metric: the professed politics of those reporting the news. Two recent studies, in the UK and the US, demonstrate increased political homogeneity within our press corps. According to the Reuters Institute for the Study of Journalism, in 2015 roughly half of British journalists identified with the political left. But by 2023, more than three-quarters did so.[9] *The American Journalist* study, meanwhile, found that while in 1971, 25.7 per cent of full-time journalists identified as Republicans, by 2022, just 3.4 per cent did so.[10] Former National Public Radio editor Uri Berliner touched on this same dynamic in a 2024 *Free Press* essay on how the public broadcaster had lost America's trust.[11] Concerned about a lack of viewpoint diversity in his own organization, Berliner tracked down the voter registration information for his newsroom, located in NPR's D.C. headquarters. He discovered eighty-seven registered Democrats in editorial positions and zero Republicans.

But the problem is not just that media workers lean decisively left. It is also, as Berliner argues, that we've lost all touch with perspectives on the right. And this lack of viewpoint diversity, combined with a lack of curiosity and critical thinking, has blinded us, causing us to make critical factual errors.

One way that newsrooms have historically resisted groupthink is to pit bias against bias in daily story meeting debates. But if no one holds alternate views, no moderating forces are present, and the collective adoption of more extreme stances can occur. According to a study published in the *American Political Science Review*,[12] this is not unique to our industry; partisan echo chambers, or 'the political homogeneity of people's social environment', reliably increases both policy preference polarization and affective polarization, defined as 'an emotional attachment to the in-group party and hostility toward the out-group party', compared to discussions among more politically mixed groups. In the case of the media, this has sometimes meant embracing identitarian moralism viewpoints that are largely out of step with the general public. 'It's true that NPR has always had a liberal bent, but during most of my tenure here, an open-minded, curious culture prevailed', Berliner wrote of his twenty-five years at the broadcaster. 'We were nerdy, but not knee-jerk, activist, or scolding'. In recent years, he argued, that has changed. 'Today, those who listen to NPR or read its coverage online find something different: the distilled worldview of a very small segment of the U.S. population'. This has resulted in coverage that's not just ideological, but also increasingly tedious and off-putting, even to those who would normally be sympathetic. Including Berliner himself – who was raised by a lesbian peace activist mother and has said he 'fit the NPR mold' – and, as it turns out, me.

In a piece for UnHerd, 'Escaping American tribalism',[13] the acclaimed essayist William Deresiewicz wrote about his lifelong love of NPR, which he discovered at the age of 23 and previously described as 'my home in America'. For thirty years, he wrote, it was 'the soundtrack of my life – when I drove, cooked, ate, exercised, did laundry – three or four hours a day, every day'.

But during the unrest of 2020, that changed. 'It was clear from the beginning that the network would be covering the movement not like journalists but advocates', Deresiewicz maintained.

> Every segment was about race, and when it wasn't about race, it was about gender. The stories were no longer reports but morality plays, with predictable bad guys and good guys. Skepticism was banished. Divergent opinions were banished. The pronouncements of activists, the arguments of ideologically motivated academics, were accepted without question. The tone became smug, certain, self-righteous. To turn on the network was to be subjected to a program of ideological force-feeding.

But this approach has consequences, Deresiewicz told me.[14] To function, society needs 'as accurate a picture as possible of reality'.

This is the crux of it: when journalists become political actors focused on political outcomes, they are in danger of ignoring, dismissing, or overlooking facts that challenge deeply held beliefs – and, as a result, they risk getting stories wrong. This was the case, Berliner wrote, in NPR's coverage of high-profile stories like the Trump campaign's potential collusion with Russia in the first election (the Mueller report, in Berliner's words, later 'found no credible evidence of collusion', with the *Columbia Journalism Review* publishing a 24,000-word piece on the industry's reporting errors during that period). It was also true of stories like the contents of Hunter Biden's laptop as Russian disinformation (the *Washington Post* and other outlets later confirmed the legitimacy of thousands of emails) and the conviction that the lab leak theory on the origin of the pandemic was a debunked conspiracy theory (it has since been deemed worthy of investigation by multiple US governmental agencies, and in 2025 the CIA stated, albeit with 'low confidence', that a 'research-related origin' was 'more likely than a natural origin based on the available body of reporting'[15]). Given such mistakes, and the network's reticence to reckon with them in public, it's perhaps not surprising that a Harris Poll that Berliner referenced found that just three in ten Americans familiar with NPR deemed it trustworthy.

This result is not, it turns out, an anomaly. In fact, it is in line with a trend that Azim Shariff, a professor at the University of British Columbia in Canada, has uncovered in research. The social psychologist, along with the American behavioural scientist Cory Clark and a group of colleagues, found that the public loses trust in institutions when they are perceived as politicized – specifically when people's politics appear to be influencing their work. (The pre-print paper[16] cites an interesting example: according to research from Floyd Zhang, published in the *Nature Human Behaviour* journal,[17] when the scientific journal *Nature* endorsed Joe Biden for president, the move resulted in not just a measurable loss of trust in *Nature* among Trump supporters, but also a loss of trust in scientists in general.) Among the more surprising findings of Shariff's research was that people lose trust when institutions become politicized – even when their politics happen to align with those of the institution. 'Even when it's your own side', Shariff stressed to me, 'you lose trust if you see it politicized'.[18]

Taking all of this into account, a picture emerges of a press that's working against its own best interests by disproportionately focusing on progressive narratives. And perhaps the most persuasive evidence that the media has indeed been overly preoccupied with identitarian moralism comes from Stony Brook University journalism professor Musa al-Gharbi. With David Rozado and Jamin Halberstadt, he analysed 27 million news and opinion articles, drawn from forty-seven popular outlets over fifty years.[19] They discovered a marked increase in the use of terms signalling prejudice towards gender, ethnicity, religion, and sexual orientation, starting around 2010 and accelerating after 2015.

If we can accept that progressive politics have played a considerable role in our coverage, then we should also admit that, as culturally dominant as this set of preoccupations has been, its proponents are, as Berliner pointed out, concentrated in a relatively small demographic. In a recent national survey called 'Hidden tribes',[20] for instance, the anti-polarization non-profit More in Common found that progressive activists, defined as 'younger, highly engaged, secular, cosmopolitan, angry', amounted to 8 per cent of the population and had the highest socio-economic and education levels of all seven categories in the report. Pew Research Center, meanwhile, examined nine categories,[21] and found this demographic to be even smaller. The progressive left, which it described as 'very liberal, highly educated and majority White', constituted about 6 per cent of the population and 7 per cent of the voting public. (This dynamic was illustrated in a humorous way in the *New York Times* in the summer of 2020 when Oregon resident Seyi Fasoranti told the paper, 'There are more Black Lives Matter signs in Portland than Black people'.[22])

In her latest book, *Outclassed: How the Left Lost the Working Class and How to Win Them Back*,[23] the University of California law professor Joan C. Williams provided extensive data demonstrating that progressives are, in many ways, outliers. For instance, progressive activists are far less patriotic than their countrymen; in fact, they are 'about three times more likely than the average American to say that they are ashamed to be an American'. Progressives are also less religious, chillier towards gun owners, more concerned about climate change, and more supportive of affirmative action. The same dynamic holds for issues as diverse as the distribution of wealth (Americans largely favour 'predistribution', or labour market interventions, but progressives support redistribution through taxes) and speech norms (between two-thirds and 100 per cent of other groups see political correctness as a problem, but just about a third of progressives do). 'Very often, college educated elites, they really just don't understand two things', Williams told me.[24] 'They don't understand that people who aren't elite are different than they are, and they can't see the water that they swim in. They can't see that their own truths are parochial, and that privileged lives give rise to privileged truths. And blue-collar lives give rise to a very different set of central concerns.'

The Canadian scholar Eric Kaufmann, who is based in England, reports similar findings for Canada. In a survey study for the Macdonald-Laurier Institute, 'The politics of the culture wars in contemporary Canada',[25] he found that the majority of Canadians rejected the views of progressive activists. For instance, 70 per cent rejected the idea that Canada was a racist country, 70 per cent preferred a colour-blind approach to society over identity politics, 85 per cent opposed teaching children 'there is no such thing as biological sex, only gender preference', and 78 per cent said that 'political correctness has gone too far'.

If only a small number of North Americans hold progressive activist beliefs, and these beliefs are disproportionately represented in our media, it follows that the public would lose basic faith in its ability to accurately reflect reality – even if this was not read as politicization, and even if did not result in reporting errors, which it clearly has.

It's also worth considering another, more complex factor at play here: while progressive activists claim to represent society's underprivileged – and no doubt many are very sincere in their beliefs – the movement itself is, as we have seen, largely made up of educated knowledge workers. During the mass demonstrations of 2020, for instance, the *New York Times* reported research findings that 82 per cent of white protesters had a college degree, while 67 per cent of Black protesters did.[26] Critically, many of these educated knowledge workers, as Vanessa Grigoriadis foretold in her *New York* piece almost two decades ago, were struggling with rising economic precarity, and, as a result, with thwarted life ambitions.

In his critically acclaimed 2024 book *We Have Never Been Woke: The Cultural Contradictions of a New Elite*, Musa al-Gharbi explored the impact of such struggles. The sociologist and *Guardian* columnist made a compelling case that periods of social justice–styled unrest have occurred several times in the past century and are in fact about 'frustrated erstwhile elites condemning the social order that failed them and jockeying to secure the position they feel they "deserve"'.[27]

Raised in Sierra Vista, Arizona, in a military family, al-Gharbi had sold shoes for a living before being accepted to graduate school at Columbia University. His move to the Upper West Side of Manhattan produced a form of 'cultural whiplash', he told me on my podcast.[28] He was particularly troubled by what he saw as an observable but little remarked upon race- and class-based caste system that involved urban knowledge professionals, or symbolic capitalists in his parlance, outsourcing the grunt work of their daily lives – from grocery shopping and meals to navigating gridlock – to an underclass of poorly paid and often desperate workers exploited by apps.

Yet this same group of knowledge workers was preoccupied with social justice politics. The contradiction was puzzling.

When Donald Trump was elected, al-Gharbi's Columbia classmates, overwhelmingly from affluent backgrounds, were so distressed that they wept in class and expressed fears for their children's safety. A common complaint was that Trump was unabashedly against the marginalized and in favour of society's elites, he told me. 'Well, guess what? We're the elites.' Meanwhile, the school's employees, often low-income immigrants, showed up to work as usual. 'They were the same people that the students viewed as being most vulnerable to Trump's regime', he told me. 'But there was no movement to help the janitors and the landscapers and the cafeteria workers and the construction people'.

All of this caused al-Gharbi to wonder if the post-2010 phenomenon popularly referred to as the Great Awokening was far more complicated than generally understood. He came to believe that it was, in fact, 'a *case* of something'. And that it occurred in 'moments of strong socioeconomic insecurity' for symbolic capitalists, such as in the 1930s, in the Great Depression, which followed a decade of significant increases in enrolment at institutions of higher education. Al-Gharbi wrote in his book that 'suddenly, many who had taken for granted a position among the elite, who had felt more or less entitled to a secure, respected, and well-paying professional job, found themselves facing deeply uncertain futures – especially because layered on top of the economic insecurity were profound geopolitical concerns'. A draft for the Second World War was on the horizon (and indeed was implemented in 1940), and 'the anxiety, frustration, and looming socioeconomic humiliation of elite aspirants quickly curdled into rage against existing elites and the society that failed them'. In *We Have Never Been Woke*, Al-Gharbi pointed to a revealing college magazine editorial from the time: 'Educated for jobs that do not materialize, students will grow resentful towards the existing order and will use the learning they have acquired to overthrow it'.[29]

Readers might be surprised to discover, as I was, that students across America joined nascent protest movements back then, supporting causes ranging from civil rights and feminism to gay rights, socialism, and anti-war opposition, as chronicled in a 1993 outing by Robert Cohen, *When the Old Left Was Young: Student Radicals and America's First Mass Student Movement, 1929–1941*.[30] Critically, though, the core demands of the 1930s students, al-Gharbi noted in his book, ranged from job placement assistance and avoidance of the draft to greater free speech freedoms on campus, 'all quite reasonable things to desire – but they are not exactly altruistic'. The subsequent crackdowns on student unrest served to reinforce young people's sense that 'the ruling class was corrupt, out of touch, unable to rise to the moment, and in need of replacement (by people like themselves)'. Significantly, by the time FDR ran for re-election in 1936, with the New Deal underway, the context had shifted.

Al-Gharbi maintains that that basic pattern was repeated in the mid-1960s in the face of an economic downturn, a 'surge in college enrollments' increasing competition, and expansion of the draft for the Vietnam War, tapering off in the early 1970s after President Nixon ended conscription and the economy began to recover. (Al-Gharbi argues that the Great Awokening and the Civil Rights movement are not synonymous, and that Civil Rights had already achieved many of its victories, such as *Brown v Board of Education* in 1954, and had 'begun to *lose* momentum' before the nationwide student demonstrations took hold.) A Great Awokening happened again, to a lesser degree, in the late 1980s and early 1990s, in the wake of government austerity triggering rising tuition rates, an influx of international students increasing competition at colleges and in the labour market, and numerous economic shocks: 'It was a bleak picture: aspiring symbolic capitalists had to go into more debt to get professional jobs, for which competition had grown much fiercer. Those who managed to land work had less job security, higher workloads and lower pay relative to previous years.'[31] Which brings us to the current Awokening, which started in the early 2010s, also involved a flood of new college grads and a lack of good-paying jobs for them, as well as enormous economic blows, including the pandemic.

These eruptions, critically, occurred when society was producing more young people who harboured expectations of affluence and influence than could be accommodated, a trend of 'elite overproduction' that Peter Turchin explored in his 2023 book, *End Times: Elites, Counter-Elites and the Path of Political Disintegration.*[32] (Interestingly, the scholar predicted the unrest of 2020 back in 2010, based on data analysis.) 'When you have growing numbers of people who did all the right things but are just not able to live that life that they envisioned for themselves, what they tend to do is grow really frustrated with the prevailing order', al-Gharbi told me on my podcast in 2024.[33] 'They start condemning the system that they think failed them. And they try to basically tear it down – or they purport to try to tear it down. And basically, try to indict the people who are successful, the people who are currently in charge, and try to remove some of those people and create space for themselves.' In ordinary times, the general public is not particularly sympathetic to the plight of these frustrated elites, he said, since times that are good for elites are bad for regular people, and vice versa. But there are moments in history when conditions happen to be poor for both groups, and this is when Great Awokenings take place, as frustrated elites gain power and influence, backed by large numbers of frustrated 'normies' demanding change.

Why, though, does this rebellion take on a distinctly 'social justicey flavour'? Because, al-Gharbi explained to me, the symbolic professions (including, of course, journalism), have, since their inception, validated their favoured role in society through claims to serve the greater good in general and the most vulnerable in particular. In journalism's case, think of the famed credo of comforting the afflicted and afflicting the comfortable. By painting oneself as the best advocate for the marginalized, al-Gharbi said, one can legitimize one's own social standing. Conversely, one can delegitimize rivals by levying accusations of offences towards the marginalized, such as racism or sexism or homophobia. In this way, social justice rhetoric is recruited for inter-elite competition – into what are, essentially, highly charged status games. (Importantly, in al-Gharbi's reading, the anti-woke media that emerged in the Biden era is often driven by the same impulses as the woke media.)

Columbia University is, of course, on the extreme end of the spectrum, given the levels of wealth and influence that many of its graduates still enjoy. But it's essential to note, as al-Gharbi does, that the members of the symbolic capitalist class that he's identified vary greatly, encompassing not just Columbia grads destined for the *New York Times* but freelancers earning $200 an article, who may not have family wealth or connections to fall back on. And while we can and should be critical of the excesses of aspiring elites of all backgrounds, we can still retain basic sympathy for the human pain that underlies such excesses. Generations were told that if they went to school, got a job, worked hard, and respected the law, they could make a decent living, own a home, and have children if they chose. That is simply no longer the case for many young people. Grief over the failure to start a family in particular cuts to the very heart of what it means to be human, and represents a significant collapse in our social contract. And while it's important to say that the working class has obviously felt this collapse far more acutely, as evidenced by the tragic rise in deaths of despair, college graduates are not themselves immune. Instead of falling into hopelessness, they lash out in anger.

In the context of these drastically different reactions, it makes sense that one of the telltale signs of a Great Awokening, in al-Gharbi's reading, is that it produces polarization. What typically happens during these eras, he explained to me, is that elites become far more radical, while the views of ordinary citizens change little, and so what is already a gulf opens up further. 'On dataset after dataset, question after question', al-Gharbi writes in his book, 'this same pattern emerges: a rapidly growing polarization between highly educated white liberals and virtually everyone else in society from 2011 through 2021'.[34] Joan C. Williams's analysis in *Outclassed*, as we've seen, highlights similar findings. This all offers a convincing explanation for why those reporting the news and those reading it now hold dramatically different views. And al-Gharbi noted that The Media Insight Project's 2021 report 'A new way of looking at trust in media: Do Americans share journalism's core values?' found that such a gap significantly undermines trust.[35] (One of those differing views, by the way, has to do with approaches to reporting itself. Al-Gharbi pointed out that, according to Pew Research, 76 per cent of Americans think that journalists 'should always strive to give every side equal coverage', whereas only 44 per cent of journalists express that belief.[36])

It's worth lingering a moment on this polarization between the media and the public, which of course occurred in the context of an already highly polarized society, divided as it is between left and right. As overall American political polarization has intensified, the culture has arguably moved into what researchers commonly refer to as high conflict, or intractable conflict. Amanda Ripley, the author of *High Conflict: Why We Get Trapped and How We Get Out*,[37] has investigated this phenomenon extensively, in contexts as diverse as gang warfare in Chicago and political violence in Colombia. She defines high conflict as a struggle that escalates to the point where the facts no longer matter, and the fight takes on a life of its own. 'It becomes all about the fear of the other side', she told me.[38]

In this scenario, an 'us versus them' mentality pervades, and the brain behaves differently. Black-and-white thinking sets in, everything becomes oversimplified, and each side becomes increasingly baffled by the other. In this charged atmosphere, curiosity falls by the wayside, existing biases intensify, and lots of mistakes are made. Each side imitates the behaviour of the other without being aware of it, perpetually escalating the conflict and increasing the likelihood of violence. The conflict becomes magnetic, making it extremely hard to break free. In the end, 'everybody suffers in high conflict', Ripley told me.

The dynamics of high conflict in American culture are, of course, particularly pronounced online, where, in recent years, we have witnessed the rise of online mobs intent on stripping people of their reputations and livelihoods. In the 2023 book, *The Canceling of the American Mind: How Cancel Culture Undermines Trust, Destroys Institutions, and Threatens Us All*,[39] Greg Lukianoff and Rikki Schlott provided case study after case study that demonstrated that cancel culture had become a common tactic on both the left and the right, that it was a threat to individuals and organizations, and that it ultimately undermined trust in institutions. Lukianoff, who is the president of the Foundation for Individual Rights and Expression, told me that in more than two decades of work with the non-profit, he had never seen the culture so censorious.[40] 'I can't find a period since McCarthyism where you're looking at these kind of numbers', he said. 'I find it somewhat frustrating to have to continue to argue that this is happening at all, when I think all of us saw it with our own eyes.'

Journalists have certainly not been invulnerable to this censoriousness, nor to the tribal, 'us versus them' thinking behind it. And many cancellations have involved participation from members of the media, who have taken to Twitter to publicly berate and shame their colleagues. The former *New York Times* reporter Nellie Bowles, who went on to found *The Free Press* outlet with her wife Bari Weiss, wrote about this destructive dynamic in her book, *Morning After the Revolution: Dispatches from the Wrong Side of History*, detailing how she was a participant in cancel culture, and later, a target. In her telling, the political culture at the *Times* was such that a new guard of staffers 'entered the building on a mission'. These colleagues 'weren't there to tell dry news factoids so much as wield the pen for justice'.

Once she began dating Weiss, herself non grata in the news-room, Bowles told me[41] that she fell out of the good graces of fellow staffers. As she recounted in her book, 'the shift was so fast it left me dizzy'; on one occasion over drinks, a disapproving editor went so far as to refer to Weiss, who is Jewish, as a 'fucking Nazi'.[42] Complicating matters further, Bowles found herself unable to suppress her innate curiosity about the explosive cultural moment and its many contradictions. She eventually ventured into reporting territory that was considered outside the window of acceptable inquiry – not, she stressed to me, with newsroom leaders, but with the paper's increasingly powerful rank and file.

One such story took place in June of 2020, when police abolition activists took over six blocks in Seattle, after clashes led to the evacuation of the East Precinct police station and the establishment of what became known as the Capitol Hill Autonomous Zone (CHAZ). Much of the mainstream media coverage at the time uncritically repeated then mayor Jenny Durkan's characterization of the CHAZ as having 'a block party atmosphere' that presented 'no threat' to the public. Durkan even mused to CNN that the CHAZ might spark a 'summer of love'. For its part, the network reported a 'festival' feel there, complete with free food, medical tents, and movies.[43] The *Guardian* lauded the CHAZ for 'offering a real-world example of what a community can look like without police',[44] and PBS described the area's community gardens as an 'edible act of resistance'.[45]

What Nellie Bowles encountered was much different. For her *Times* piece, 'Abolish the police? Those who survived the chaos in Seattle aren't so sure',[46] Bowles interviewed Faizel Khan, a gay coffee shop owner, who, together with other small business operators from the area, was suing the city for abandoning them. Khan reported masked looters, property damage, intimidation from gun-toting white protesters, blocked access to his business, non-responsive 911 calls, lost revenue, and mounting costs for private security. After four people were shot, and two died, police ultimately regained control of the area in early July. Some of the other local business owners Bowles spoke to described having been followed by protesters wielding baseball bats, demonstrators demanding fealty to their cause, break-ins, an attempted robbery and arson, a live-streamed confrontation with a crowd of protesters, harassing phone calls, and death threats. Suffice it to say, this reporting represented a significant challenge to the dominant narrative about the Seattle experiment.

After the piece came out, Bowles told me that people she worked with at the *Times* began posting nasty tweets about her. Colleagues mocked her, circulating photos of her as a teen at a debutante ball, sourced from her private Facebook page. 'I was just getting very embarrassed', she told me. It eventually became clear, she said, that if she continued at the paper, pursuing the same reporting path, 'I was going to be badly smeared at some point, I could just feel it.'

But looking back, it was resisting an online mobbing that ultimately sealed her fate. In June of 2020, during widespread unrest, the *Times* opinion section under the leadership of James Bennet published a controversial op-ed from Senator Tom Cotton, 'Send in the troops',[47] calling for 'an overwhelming show of force'. The paper's staff revolted, posting critical tweets and penning a letter to management questioning the

decision to run the piece, which resulted in Bennet's oust-
ing. When Bowles declined to join an internet pile-on against
the editors involved,[48] the newsroom hostility towards her
increased.

And not only her. The incident, as we'll see, proved to be a
watershed in American journalism.

4

A Leadership Vacuum

Every generation of journalists has a defining moment. For the current generation, that moment is the death of George Floyd, captured by a teenaged bystander in a gut-wrenching video on 25 May 2020. When the images hit the internet, they shocked the country – and indeed the world – uniting people of all political stripes and sparking some of the largest, most multiracial, and most hopeful demonstrations in American history. As the days wore on, though, tensions escalated. Other videos began to circulate online, showing police wielding tear gas and batons. In some places, protests erupted into rioting, arson, and looting. A dozen people died in the first week and a half. The nation's initial optimism gave way to something else, something far more combustible. 'It was like all hell broke loose', Michael Powell, formerly of the *New York Times* and now of the *Atlantic*, told me.[1] 'I mean, all hell broke loose in the culture, but also within the newsroom.'

Ten days after Floyd's death, the *Times*'s opinion section published the now infamous op-ed by Tom Cotton, in which the Republican senator from Arkansas referenced violence against the police in St. Louis, Las Vegas, and New York State. Given that officers had been shot and run over by cars, he argued that a powerful military response was necessary 'to disperse, detain and ultimately deter lawbreakers'.[2] The piece proved explosive, not least within the paper itself. Within hours, *Times* journalists took to Twitter to argue that publishing it put Black staff in physical danger.

A thousand staff members signed a letter addressed to management, including to James Bennet, the head of the opinion section. Bennet believed it was important to hear from Cotton and tweeted that the outlet had an obligation to show its readers 'counter-arguments, particularly those made by people in a position to set policy'.[3] But the paper's staff disagreed. 'Although his piece specifically refers to looters as the targets of military action', the letter read, 'his proposal would no doubt encourage further violence. Invariably, violence, official and unofficial, disproportionately hurts black and brown people. It also jeopardizes our journalists' ability to work safely and effectively on the streets'.[4]

The NewsGuild of New York was involved in organizing the letter. 'I was a shop steward in the union', Powell, who did not sign the letter, recalled in an interview on my podcast in 2024.[5] 'I argued that this was antithetical to journalism. That an op-ed page in particular – and, in particular, frankly, at a liberal paper like the *New York Times* – that it was incredibly important to hear from people like Tom Cotton. Even if you 100 per cent disagree with him.'

'I have a lot of respect for A.G. Sulzberger', Powell told me, in reference to the paper's publisher, 'and for Dean Baquet, who was, I think, largely a terrific editor. But I did think in that moment they came up short. And that there was a need to express the importance of values. There was a need to stand up to that tide.'

Instead, *Times* management backed down, saying that the column failed to meet editorial standards and affixing a lengthy editor's note to the piece, explaining that the process had been rushed, should have paid more attention to 'factual questions', and had not sufficiently involved senior editors. Adam Rubenstein, the editor who handled the column, later contested this explanation in the *Atlantic*,[6] writing that 'it wasn't rushed', that 'senior editors were deeply involved', and that 'there were no correctable errors'.

Erik Wemple has characterized the *Times* controversy as 'one of the most consequential journalism fights in decades'.[7] Writing in the *Washington Post* more than two years after the uproar had died down, he blasted the editorial note, which apologized for 'non-factual issues', and remarked that 'a more pathetic collection of 317 words would be difficult to assemble'. The respected *Post* media critic, who joined the *Times* in the fall of 2025, also took the staff's Twitter protest to task. 'It was an exercise in manipulative hyperbole brilliantly calibrated for immediate impact', he wrote. 'The Erik Wemple Blog has asked about thirty *Times* staffers whether they still believe their "danger" tweets . . . Not one of them replied with an on-the-record defense.'

His own criticism, Wemple acknowledged, came 875 days too late. It was, he wrote, 'long past time to ask why more people who claim to uphold journalism and free expression – including, um, the Erik Wemple Blog – didn't speak out then in Bennet's defense'. Wemple's explanation was nothing short of breathtaking: 'It's because we were afraid to.'

Indeed, few journalists summoned the courage to defend Bennet, who was forced to resign, or Rubenstein, who eventually left. In an open letter[8] five weeks after Bennet's departure, Bari Weiss, who had worked under him, explained why she, too, was leaving: 'Showing up for work as a centrist at an American newspaper should not require bravery.' Weiss argued that the lessons that should have been learned from Trump's election – 'lessons about the importance of understanding other Americans, the necessity of resisting tribalism, and the centrality of the free exchange of ideas to a democratic society' – had simply not been learned. 'Stories that are inconvenient to the progressive political project are overlooked or ignored or explained away', she later told me.[9] 'And I think that is doing an incredible disservice to readers.'

By the end of 2021, the industry had been shaken by months of internal newsroom revolts. The editor of *Bon Appetit* resigned over an old Halloween costume; the editor of *Refinery29* resigned over accusations of a toxic workplace; the editor of *Variety* was placed on leave for calling a freelancer 'bitter' on Twitter; the newly hired editor of *Teen Vogue*, Alexi McCammond, resigned before starting the job, after offensive tweets she'd sent as a teenager enraged its staff. Lee Fang, a reporter for *The Intercept*, was reportedly 'hauled before H.R.' for posting an interview[10] with a Black Lives Matter protester who questioned why Black lives only mattered when it was white men who killed them, because the sentiment was deemed racist by one of Fang's colleagues. 'I couldn't believe they were coming for the man's job over something I said', the Oakland protester, Max, told Matt Taibbi.[11] 'It was not Lee's opinion. It was my opinion.'

This all did not take place without at least some resistance from within the press corps. Andy Mills told me that in the wake of the Tom Cotton scandal, he and a group of *Times* colleagues came together.[12] He said they disagreed with the 'small but mighty group' who rejected the idea that journalism was 'a place for us to understand each other better' and instead saw it as 'essentially a tool of power that we should use to push the right political views, and in many cases the right moral views, on the public'. The *Times* group began meeting regularly, discussing how to prevent an incident like the Cotton affair from ever happening again. 'Sadly', he said, 'we had not figured out the answer to that question by the time I myself was caught in a scandal'.

As Mills told Katie Herzog on the *Blocked and Reported* podcast,[13] he had grown up in a town in Illinois with just a thousand residents, an evangelical Christian. While he'd initially planned to become a minister, at college he grappled with doubts and became uncomfortable with the idea of telling people what to believe. Attracted to the idea of learning about people's lives and experiences, he pursued journalism instead. After doing a year-long print journalism research contract in what is now South Sudan, he failed to land a full-time media job and began painting houses. As he listened to *This American Life* episodes all day painting, he found himself captivated by the medium's storytelling. So, he bought a microphone and got a friend to teach him how to edit audio. Mills began crafting audio pieces in his spare time, as he worked in bars and coffee shops and factories. After winning an industry award for one such audio piece, he was recruited by the public radio show *Radiolab*, moved to New York, and went on to become one of the industry's most celebrated audio talents.

But in the early 2010s, as a production assistant at *Radiolab*, Mills was accused of unprofessional conduct.[14] His transgressions included referring to colleagues as 'gals', an unsolicited backrub, and, in a more serious incident, dumping a drink on a co-worker at a bar. Though he had been disciplined for these actions at the time and had been open with the *Times* about his history in 2016 when he joined the paper, the incidents were dredged up again in 2018 by *New York Magazine*, in the context of a much broader investigation into workplace culture at WNYC studios, where *Radiolab* was produced.[15] The accusations resurfaced again in 2020 on Twitter, by the colleague from the bar incident, in the fallout from a scandal surrounding a *Times* podcast, *Caliphate*. Mills and his team had returned a Peabody Award after a central subject of the show was arrested in Canada, and charged with a terrorism hoax, later admitting his claims were false,[16] thereby collapsing some of the reporting on the show. There was a feeling on Twitter that while *Caliphate* host Rukmini Callimachi had been reassigned, Mills remained on the popular *Times* podcast *The Daily*, and was thriving there, which was considered unfair. What began as a critique of race relations – why did a white male suffer no professional consequences for a major journalistic mistake? – soon morphed into a critique based around another hot-button issue: gender.

Mills told me that the narrative on social media quickly escalated, with strangers on social media referring to him as a sexual predator and claiming that his presence made staff unsafe. It was an incredibly confusing and painful thing to go through, he said. On the one hand, it was 'devastatingly embarrassing' to see his interpersonal missteps once again aired out in the public square. He deeply regretted his behaviour from years earlier, particularly the drink incident. On the other hand, much of the accusations online were 'completely untrue and exaggerated and increased in its velocity by the telephone game of Twitter'. Several weeks prior he had been promoted, to the audio department's director of development, and he said zero new information about his conduct had surfaced since then. ('Andy was very unfairly treated', Ben Smith, a former *Times* media columnist, recently said on Mills's podcast, *Reflector*.[17])

At the same time as this was going on, the acclaimed reporter Donald McNeil Jr, a forty-five-year veteran of the *Times* who had worked his way up from a copy boy, was himself facing a scandal. He had become, in the pandemic, as Ben Smith put it in the *Times*, 'the voice of the Times's coverage of the crisis', and was up for a Pulitzer Prize. But back in 2019, he had participated in a *Times*-sponsored youth trip to Peru that led to controversy. (In his reporting of the ensuing scandal in 2021,[18] Ben Smith noted that these trips had been 'complicated to manage' and that reporters were not 'always ready for the confident, hot house politics of elite American high school students'.) During McNeil's two weeks talking with teens about public health in the Andes, he got into a series of conversations that touched on race relations. Notably, when one student described a situation in which a classmate had been suspended for using the N-word in a video she'd made in eighth grade, and McNeil attempted to ascertain the details, he uttered the actual word, which resulted in complaints from students, as well as allegations that he'd stereotyped African American teens. He, like Mills, had already been disciplined for the incident. But in the turbulent pandemic era, the story leaked to *The Daily Beast*,[19] leading to coverage in other outlets. In a letter to *Times* editor Dean Baquet, which also leaked,[20] 150 *Times* employees said that staffers were 'outraged and in pain', and raised objections that McNeil had been allowed 'a prominent platform' to cover the pandemic, 'a critical beat' that was 'disproportionately affecting people of color'. The prominent *Times* journalist Nikole Hannah-Jones told *Slate*[21] that a group of Black employees asked for a call with Dean Baquet and other masthead management, but that she didn't sign the letter and didn't call for McNeil to be fired, instead asking for more transparency from the paper: 'I don't take lightly anyone losing their career over a single incident.'

Amid the Twitter firestorm, in a multi-part piece published on *Medium*[22] after he left the *Times*, McNeil acknowledged uttering the N-word but disputed many of the students' allegations and argued that the *Times* had 'panicked' and that the paper had become a vengeful place. 'It's been quite baffling and painful for me to have people assume I'm a racist and believe that I said the ridiculous things I'm accused of saying', he wrote. Mills and McNeil, both at the top of their games professionally, were forced to resign, with editor Dean Baquet telling them they'd lost the newsroom.

The free speech organization PEN America released a statement[23] saying that while it acknowledged the N-word was uniquely hurtful, 'for reporter Donald McNeil to end his long career, apparently as a result of a single word, risks sending a chilling message'. Meanwhile, Bret Stephens penned a column, spiked by the *Times* but later published in the *New York Post*, linking the incident to the broader cancel culture. 'We are living in a period of competing moral certitudes, of people who are awfully sure they're right and fully prepared to be awful about it', Stephens wrote.[24] 'The role of good journalism should be to lead us out of this dark defile.'

The context of these incidents – and their impacts on the profession as whole, let alone public trust – was not something that the media spent much time on. 'One of the things that was frustrating and painful was that this is happening at the end of 2020', Mills told me on my podcast in 2024.[25] Public shamings were increasingly more frequent during the remote work era when increased social media use was common. This was, in fact, a huge story. And yet, Mills said, 'when this thing that was happening to me, which was a textbook social media public shaming, and I got calls from people in the media, who cover the media, there was no desire on the part of these reporters to talk about the bigger picture of what was happening'.

One of the overlooked factors, which has become increasingly clear since that period, is the mixed motivations of the journalists carrying out those public shamings, which often involved at least some element of opportunism. *Atlantic* staff writer Thomas Chatterton Williams touched on this dynamic in his recent book, *Summer of Our Discontent: The Age of Certainty and the Demise of Discourse*.[26] 'I think that very quickly, people's righteous sense of moral clarity became entangled with their own career ambitions and sense of what might be owed to them', he told me.[27] So-called 'woke' politics, he said, essentially acted as a vehicle to redistribute access to success: 'If socialism or Marxism is the redistribution of capital, wokeness is the redistribution of recognition.' These public pile-ons, after all, often vacated top spots in the media. And this was surely not lost on those participating, who frequently framed their complaints in ways that betrayed their own career frustrations.

You can see this dynamic in many of the case studies of media-related cancellation campaigns. For instance, when the

New York Times food writer Alison Roman found herself in the crosshairs in May of 2020. During the stay-at-home orders early in the pandemic, the food writer had seen her star rise, as the locked-down masses rediscovered home cooking. But then she gave an interview to an online publication, *The New Consumer*,[28] and in the process, criticized two Asian lifestyle personalities, Chrissy Teigen and Marie Kondo, for launching product lines. The backlash online alleging racism was swift and brutal, and Roman's *Times* column was put on hold, with Roman eventually leaving the paper. It is telling that outraged journalists were especially aggrieved by Roman's material success. 'I love when a slightly off center but nevertheless extremely popular social media figure declares she is not making much money right now and no one questions it', the writer Lauren Oyler tweeted in the midst of the pile-on that curtailed Roman's career.[29] 'What was your book advance, what were your royalties, you sold a TV show, how much is your speaking fee?'

This returns us to our earlier discussion of intra-elite status games within the media, and the background conditions of widespread economic and professional precarity that lead to deep frustrations. 'I think cancelling somebody, or lashing out at somebody online, comes from a place of powerlessness – or at least thinking that you don't have power', the author, podcaster, and former *Los Angeles Times* columnist Meghan Daum told me.[30] 'If you can't get ahead or elevate yourself or help yourself through the normal channels, you're going to lash out at somebody and try to bring them down instead of bringing yourself up.'

Given that we are talking here about elite status competition, and a mode of politics that serves to gatekeep for elite success, it's perhaps unsurprising that the targets of successful newsroom purges were often people who were not born of the elites and were not as well versed in its culture. Similar to Andy Mills, a former house painter, and Donald McNeil, a labour union activist, Alison Roman is not a product of the Ivy League–educated press corps, having worked her way up in restaurant kitchens, eventually lucking into a position at *Bon Appetit*.[31] As is the case with many who've spent a lot of time in working-class spaces, Roman is, by her own admission, brasher and more outspoken. These purges, for whatever else they did, ultimately served to enforce rapidly evolving elite norms.

Another underappreciated element of the newsroom purges was, as PEN predicted, the chilling effect on newsrooms across America – and beyond. Canada saw its own high-profile shake-ups, including a scandal in June 2020 involving the Canadian Broadcasting Corporation host Wendy Mesley. 'After George Floyd's murder last May, a Black CBC reporter tweeted that she had repeatedly been called the N-word', Mesley wrote in *The Globe and Mail* newspaper a year later.[32] 'I was furious. I wanted to put her on the air to discuss that, and said so in a conference call with producers for *The Week with Wendy Mesley*. During our discussion, I was so upset over what our colleague experienced that I stupidly filled in the N-Word.' Mesley maintained that she immediately apologized, but a subsequent investigation discovered another instance when she used the word – this time repeating a book title in a meeting.

Mesley was suspended and eventually parted ways with her employer of thirty-eight years. (Where she'd also worked her way up, dropping out of college after an unorthodox childhood with a single mother.[33]) 'After a year of reflection and a whole range of emotions', Mesley wrote, 'I'm left feeling mostly disappointed, because this could have been handled so differently'. She was not alone in feeling that way. Richard Stursberg, the executive vice president of CBC/Radio-Canada from 2004 to 2010, told me over coffee in 2025 that he thought the scandal was 'just ridiculous.' He wondered: 'What kind of radical purity is involved with saying you can't say the name of a book?'

Another headline-making incident involved the firing of radio host Jamil Jivani, recently elected as a Conservative member of the Canadian Parliament, and now known stateside for his close friendship with Vice President J.D. Vance. In a statement of defence[34] in the resulting wrongful dismissal suit,[35] the telecommunications giant Bell said that Jivani had failed to sufficiently push back on anti-vaccination and anti-government sentiments, declined to use the pop star Demi Lovato's preferred pronouns, and exhibited an 'open disdain' for Bell's diversity initiatives: 'The Plaintiff refused to participate in any of Bell's DEI initiatives, suggesting instead that [Bell] "demonstrate a commitment to true diversity: diversity of thought."'

Jivani, a child of a single mother, was considered illiterate as a teen, but eventually overcame his challenges to attend Yale Law School. He was hired by Bell in the summer of 2020 and told me on my podcast in 2022 that he saw the radio gig as an opportunity to showcase the wide range of perspectives within the Black community, which he felt was being overlooked by the mainstream media.[36] 'We don't all think the same', he said. 'We weren't all out there marching with Black Lives Matter – in fact, the vast majority of us were not.' Jivani said it soon became obvious that Bell had a very different approach to diversity and that arguments for a more nuanced approach seemed unwelcome in meetings. He felt the climate was not conducive to open dialogue, particularly on sensitive issues like race relations: 'I think a lot of people are scared.'

Many have since argued that the newsroom purges of 2020 did indeed create a profoundly illiberal environment. Critics include Michael Lind, a writer, professor, and co-founder of the New America think tank. 'It does remind you of the Soviet Union, or of a totalitarian state, in which you make one false statement, you make one reckless remark, and you're ratted out', Lind said when we discussed the industry.[37] 'And not to the secret police, but to the H.R. department.' It was such illiberalism that James Bennet focused on in his own account of the upheavals of 2020, in a lengthy piece for *1843*, a magazine published by *The Economist*.[38] 'The *Times*'s problem has metastasized from liberal bias to illiberal bias', he argued, 'from an inclination to favour one side of the national debate to an impulse to shut debate down altogether'.

All told, the purges of 2020 sent a strong message to journalists that if they wanted to stay employed, they had best proceed with extreme caution. But as we've seen, extreme caution does not foster a healthy newsroom culture, which requires daily debate. Without respect for disagreement, monocultures develop, and newsrooms become echo chambers with little connection to the wider public. The purges sent a signal, too, to the rank and file that leadership was more likely to appease radicals than stand up to them, and so journalists began to avoid confrontations with activist colleagues.

In this climate, an idea that had been smouldering for years caught fire. And it was this idea that finally set the trust spiral ablaze.

5

A Rejection of Objectivity

In his account of the *Times* newsroom revolt over the Tom Cotton op-ed,[1] Ben Smith, the paper's then media columnist, located the beginnings of this heightened cultural moment on 14 August 2014, in Ferguson, Missouri, where unrest had engulfed the streets after the fatal police shooting of an unarmed teen, Michael Brown. Wesley Lowery, a 24-year-old reporter with the *Washington Post*, had woken up that morning – his face aching from having been pushed into a soda machine during an arrest the night before (which he had filmed and posted online[2]) – and called in for an appearance on CNN. The host relayed advice from MSNBC's Joe Scarborough[3] that Lowery should 'move along' faster next time police issued instructions to evacuate (what was not repeated was that Scarborough had added unless his goal was 'to get on TV and have people talk about me the next day'). Lowery got angry, describing a dystopian scene on the ground and inviting Scarborough to 'get out of 30 Rock where he's sitting there sipping his Starbucks smugly' to visit Ferguson for himself. Lowery said he had 'little patience for talking heads', and fumed that this was 'a community in the United States of America, where things are on fire'. The dressing down of Scarborough earned applause on

Twitter. And in the course of Lowery's Ferguson reporting, his online following exploded.

Smith's choice of anecdote illustrated a number of themes that were simultaneously unfolding a decade or so ago: the tensions between reporters and officers; the shock that many young journalists felt encountering a militarized police force in the streets; the nascent Black Lives Matter movement, which would find many supporters among the press; and the generational shift away from deference to authority and towards a new outspokenness, turbocharged by social media.

By the summer of 2020, Lowery had become a bona fide media star and a Pulitzer Prize–winner. He'd also been disciplined by *Post* editor Marty Baron over his outspokenness on social media. Baron wrote in his memoir *Collision of Power: Trump, Bezos, and the Washington Post*[4] that he had urged the paper's managing editor to recruit Lowery – whose work showed 'impressive talent and energy' – but that Lowery's 'combative instincts' soon raised issues for management. This included the Joe Scarborough scuffle, but also various Twitter fights with detractors as well as sharp criticism of colleagues, both within the paper and in the wider media. Among the examples Baron cited: an instance in which Lowery publicly accused the media of being 'cowardly' for not immediately labelling an inflammatory Trump comment 'racist', and an instance in which Lowery mocked *New York Times* columnist Maureen Dowd as a 'decadent aristocrat'.

After five years of warnings that his online posts frequently veered into opinion, were intemperate, violated the *Post*'s code of conduct for social media, and had the ability to compromise the reputation and standards of the paper, Baron delivered a disciplinary letter to Lowery. This read, in part:

> The issue here is where and how to provide your perspective on issues facing the media, including coverage of race. You should not use social media to send messages to colleagues

in the newsroom. You should not use social media to criticize
competitors for their coverage. You should not use social media
as a forum to express what, by any reasonable reading, would
be viewed as your political opinions . . . Above all, what we ask
of you is restraint.

Lowery subsequently left the paper for a CBS News offshoot
of *60 Minutes*, tweeting, 'Should go without saying: reporters
of color shouldn't have their jobs threatened for speaking out
about mainstream media failures to properly cover and con-
textualize issues of race. What's the point of bringing diverse
experiences and voices into a room only to muzzle them?'[5]
    Several months later, when Tom Cotton's op-ed appeared,
Lowery quickly entered the fray, tweeting, 'American view-
from-nowhere, "objectivity"-obsessed, both-sides journalism
is a failed experiment . . . We need to rebuild our industry as
one that operates from a place of moral clarity.' Later that June,
he published an op-ed of his own in the *Times*, arguing that
the news business should move beyond objectivity and adopt
'a method of moral clarity'.[6]
    In the wake of the post–George Floyd racial reckoning
that was taking place across American society, and in its
streets, Lowery wrote in that 2020 *Times* essay, many Black
journalists were 'openly pushing for a paradigm shift in how
our outlets define their operations and ideals'. He argued that
while modern journalism's stated goal was to be objective,
each piece of news that was produced sat 'atop a pyramid of
subjective decision-making' – from story and source selection
to the details highlighted or downplayed – and such calls
were often made by white reporters and editors and bosses,
with the sensibility of white readers in mind. 'No journalistic
process is objective', he stressed. 'And no individual journalist
is objective, because no human being is.'
    It's true that no journalist is without biases or blind spots,
and that any set of standards and practices attempting to

mitigate this will always be imperfect. But there are some obvious problems with Lowery's formulation of moral clarity as a replacement for the traditional, albeit flawed, aspiration of objectivity. For one, it's unclear who gets to decide on the moral judgement for any given story. The writer? The editor? The publisher? The newsroom's rank and file? Social media? What happens if there is disagreement in the newsroom? Generally speaking, most people think their belief system is solid – who will be the arbiter? And what happens if facts subsequently emerge that contradict that initial judgement?

Lowery's critique also makes flawed assumptions about the correlation of race and viewpoint, assigning monolithic perspectives to both white and Black actors, and failing to take into account the vast array of other forces that shape our experiences of the world, including, among other things, age, class background, education, region, culture, family structure, religion, gender, sexual orientation, and political affiliation. Lowery assigns special powers of knowledge to skin colour alone that may or may not wind up being true, depending on the situation. Would, for instance, an Ivy League–educated Black reporter from an affluent, suburban background have a special understanding of the struggles of an impoverished, inner-city young Black man confronting the criminal justice system? Perhaps. But perhaps not, too.

It is also not clear how the 'method' for moral clarity would operate in practice. Lowery stressed accuracy and fairness and critical evaluation of sources like police departments, but these values already are (or should be) associated with traditional objectivity. He also emphasized the need to speak plainly, to have 'a more aggressive commitment to truth', and to be ethical. But these are highly subjective concepts, open to much interpretation, and thus pose obvious risks for the creep of opinion into news reporting.

Nevertheless, despite the vagueness of its formulation, there can be little doubt that the moral clarity ideal caught fire. Indeed, it would be difficult to overstate the impact of Lowery's idea. It effectively ushered in a new era – indeed a new standard – in journalism. At the *New Yorker*, Masha Gessen wrote a widely discussed essay, 'Why are some journalists afraid of "moral clarity"?'[7] Lewis Raven Wallace, who'd been fired from the public radio show *Marketplace* for penning a blog proclaiming objectivity dead, saw renewed interest in *The View from Somewhere: Undoing the Myth of Journalistic Objectivity*,[8] published the previous year. In Canada, similar calls to question the role of objectivity followed, including an award-winning *Walrus* magazine essay by Pacinthe Mattar, 'Objectivity is a privilege afforded to white journalists'.[9] The Canadian journalism professors Candis Callison and Mary Lynn Young advanced this view, too, drawing on their 2019 book *Reckoning: Journalism's Limits and Possibilities*.[10]

The moral clarity ideal was not without its critics, though. The historian David Greenberg, writing in the quarterly *Liberties*,[11] argued that 'newly fashionable phrases' like 'moral clarity' should make us pause, 'not only because they were first popularized by Bush during the war on terrorism, but also because determining the correct moral posture on a political or policy issue is almost always difficult'. It was certainly, he suggested, 'beyond the capacity of a daily journalist working at digital speed'. If we led with moral convictions before we determined what had happened, Greenberg later told me, we could get ourselves into trouble, 'Because we're always going to be wrong, no matter how virtuous or politic. Even if we believe that our own world view is fundamentally sound, sometimes the other side has a point.'[12]

George Packer, an *Atlantic* staff writer, also resisted. He told me that he was dismayed, while participating in a Columbia Journalism School panel, when objectivity was referred to as 'the O-word' and no other journalist would defend it.[13] While Packer did not reject the concept of moral clarity entirely, he believed most things were not black and white. 'Moral clarity has a way of blinding us to the nuances and the details that make it harder to make up your mind. But that's what readers have to confront: that things are difficult, that most issues are hard to make your mind about.' Packer worried that the next generation of journalists celebrated 'the freedom that comes with not having to be objective', which, he feared, could ulti-mately mean freeing oneself from 'the tyranny of facts, the tyranny of reality'. Objectivity, he noted, 'is hard work'.

And indeed, returning to the scandal on the Tom Cotton op-ed, Lowery's moral clarity framework led him to jump to the conclusion, in his own *Times* op-ed, that the incident was fairly cut and dried when it was not. Lowery wrote:

> Let's take a moment to be honest about what actually happened in this case: An op-ed page accepted an essay from a firebrand senator. It published that column without adequate line or conceptual editing. Then it got called out for it, leading to the resignation of one man in top leadership and the resignation of another. It was a rare case of accountability.

Yet, as we've seen in these pages, this conclusion was hotly contested by a number of former *Times* staffers. Crucially, the central fact Lowery relies on to make his case – that the *Times* piece was published without adequate editorial oversight – has been disputed by the editors involved, in pieces for the *Atlantic* and the *Economist.* Lowery's own deployment of the moral clarity model, then, produced an oversimplified and potentially inaccurate depiction of a complex and consequential story.

Still, the traditional method of objectivity does appear to have fallen out of favour with the press corps, at least according to a 2023 piece in the *Washington Post*[14] by the celebrated former *Post* editor Leonard Downie Jr, who worked on the Watergate story and is now a journalism professor. With fellow professor and former CBS News president Andrew Heyward, he interviewed more than seventy-five journalists, news leaders, and mainstream media experts to study the values and practices in modern newsrooms. Their research suggested 'the beginning of another generational shift in American journalism'. Downie noted: 'What we found has convinced us that truth-seeking news media must move beyond whatever "objectivity" once meant to produce more trustworthy news.'

The objectivity debate, as Greenberg pointed out in his *Liberties* essay, is not a new one. It is hardly the first time that objectivity has come under attack. We can learn much from the history of the ideal, chronicled in *Discovering the News: A Social History of American Newspapers*, by the Columbia journalism professor Michael Schudson. As Schudson wrote in that landmark book, objectivity is a professional value that 'seemed to disintegrate as soon as it was formulated', experiencing challenges as soon as it was widely established in the early twentieth century.[15] Indeed, objectivity emerged out of an acknowledgement of a liability in journalism – the inherent subjectivity of our work – and it's been contested from day one.

The journalistic method of objectivity – a set of practices designed to separate facts from value judgements – arose in distinction to a press dominated by both commercial and political interests. The openly partisan papers of the nineteenth century were often financed by political parties and candidates. Then the penny papers followed. According to Schudson, they originated the modern conception of news through a more 'democratic attitude toward the happenings of the world', breaking away from the partisan model, generating revenue from subscriptions and advertising, and covering a wider range of topics. 'Most of the penny papers', Schudson wrote, 'including all of the pioneers in the field, claimed political independence, something that earlier papers rarely pretended to'.[16]

When Adolph Ochs bought the *New York Times* in 1896 for $75,000, he famously declared that the news should be presented 'without fear or favor'. Schudson noted that the paper 'established the standard' for this new ethos, which then spread widely in the early twentieth century, and was, as the scholar detailed, ultimately a defensive strategy. It was deployed in response to the 'skepticism and suspicion which thinkers of the late nineteenth century, like Nietzsche, taught'. That cynicism went on to 'became part of general education', and reduced the public's faith in sources of authority. Objectivity was also a response to the propaganda and distorted reporting during the First World War; Schudson notes that the *Times* described the Great War as 'the first press agents' war' and the historian Jack Roth called it 'the first modern effort at systemic, nationwide manipulation of collective passions'.[17] In *Liberty and the News*, first published in 1920, the iconic journalist Walter Lippmann described the era as one in which 'there is everywhere an increasingly angry disillusionment about the press, a growing sense of being baffled and misled'. He worried that people would 'cease to respond to truths and respond simply to opinions' and would 'believe whatever fits most comfortably with their prepossessions'.[18] As David Greenberg noted, in *Public Opinion*,[19] published in 1922, Lippmann observed that 'as our minds become more deeply aware of their own subjectivism, we find a zest in objective method that is not otherwise there'. Inspired by the era's fascination with science, a set of practices evolved that aimed to counter a reporter's natural biases and produce information that was both reliable and replicable.

In his *Liberties* essay, Greenberg provides a concise summary of these practices:

> In the reporting stage, they call for independently verifying sources' claims and talking to a mix of sources so as not to fall captive to one person's perspective. In the writing stage, they prescribe an antiseptic tone: no ideology, snark, self-righteousness, anger, euphoria, invective, or exaggeration. They call for furnishing evidence to substantiate doubtful assertions.

They stipulate the attribution of claims to let readers judge their validity. They require the inclusion of multiple, competing explanations about complex or controversial issues. Similar practices exist for editing (having multiple editors review a story); photojournalism (no staging or doctoring images); even anchoring the news (the Olympian Cronkite delivery). Large news agencies concerned with protecting their reputation for objectivity also impose rules to reassure readers that their employees approach stories with an open mind. While correspondents may offer considered judgements about the events they cover, they must not have conflicts of interest – a scruple that is a small moral revolution in itself. And they may not crusade on behalf of a cause or spout off carelessly. Doing otherwise would compromise their credibility.

Though challenges to objectivity have been ongoing since the method first emerged, the last major debate around it took place in the 1960s – and also broke down along generational lines. In that era, 'objectivity in journalism, regarded as an antidote to bias, came to be looked upon as the most insidious bias of all', Schudson wrote, with many arguing that it 'reproduced a vision of social reality which refused to examine the basic structures of power and privilege'. He pointed to a telling story in the *Wall Street Journal* in 1969, featuring a young *Raleigh Observer* reporter, Kerry Gruson, who covered the 15 October mass demonstrations against the Vietnam War wearing a black armband, and declared that 'objectivity is a myth'. Her father, Sydney Gruson, assistant to the publisher of the *New York Times*, had a very different take: 'Maybe I'm old-fashioned but I feel very strongly about the purity of news columns. Pure objectivity may not exist, but you have to strive for it anyway.'[20] The *Journal* story on anti-war activism among the young press corps reported that the senior Gruson had denied a group of more than three hundred staffers use of a company auditorium to meet for discussions about the

15 October moment, a decision that his daughter publicly disagreed with.

If the most notable push against objectivity occurred in the turbulent late 1960s and early 1970s, there have since been numerous occasions when news-gathering journalists and media thinkers have criticized it as inadequate. War correspondent Christiane Amanpour, who faced criticism over her reporting in Bosnia in the 1990s, told CNN that 'in situations of gross violations of human rights . . . you cannot be neutral because then you are an accomplice', and that the goal should be to be 'truthful, not neutral'.[21] As mentioned earlier, many in the business have also argued that objectivity's attempts at fairness can result in false balance, or 'bothsideism'. In the words of Brent Cunningham, the *Columbia Journalism Review*'s former editor, writing in 2003 in the wake of the failures in coverage around the lead-up to the Iraq War, objectivity 'often excuses lazy reporting'.[22] And in a 2017 outing, *Just a Journalist: On the Press, Life, and the Spaces Between*, the Pulitzer Prize–winning *Times* reporter Linda Greenhouse, who covered the Supreme Court for almost thirty years, recounted her own struggles with the limitations of objectivity, including controversies in 1989 around her participation in a march for reproductive rights, and in 2006, around a Harvard speech in which she made controversial comments about the Bush administration. 'As one who has long sought to understand the implications of the objectivity norm', she wrote in the book's preface, 'who has challenged it in writing and been seen to transgress it in my personal behavior, I was fascinated and thrilled by the trajectory of the 2016 campaign coverage and by the media's willingness to confront a hostile president'.[23]

Such critiques have often made important points, and the debates have been, I think, largely healthy for the profession. Many criticisms have been incorporated into the concept of objectivity, an evolution that Schudson has called Objectivity 2.0. The racial diversification of American and Canadian newsrooms, long overdue, was part of that effort. (Yet, as we've seen, just as newsrooms became more racially diverse, they became markedly less diverse in terms of class and education and geography.)

In the post–George Floyd era, the objectivity debate has become particularly explosive, in ways that have not helped us and have instead eroded public trust. In response, some of journalism's older guard have mounted a spirited defence of the ideal. Indeed, in the 2021 edition of *The Elements of Journalism: What Newspeople Should Know and the Public Should Expect*, Bill Kovach and Tom Rosenstiel argued that the method was even more critical in the digital age. 'We want to recapture the original meaning of objectivity intended when the concept migrated from social science to journalism early in the twentieth century', the authors wrote. 'Objectivity was not meant to suggest that journalists were without bias. To the contrary, precisely because journalists could never be objective, their methods had to be. In recognition that everyone is biased, in other words, the news, like science, should flow from a process for reporting that is defensible, rigorous, and transparent'.[24]

The publisher of the *New York Times*, A.G. Sulzberger, offered a similarly strong defence of the ideal in the *Columbia Journalism Review*,[25] albeit rebranding objectivity as independence. 'The model of journalistic independence is explicitly designed to help correct for the narrowness of a journalist's own experience and worldview, including by intentionally seeking out and attempting to fairly convey a much broader range of views', he wrote. 'It doesn't deny personal experience; it provides a method not to be trapped by it.' He noted elsewhere in the piece that

> independence asks reporters to adopt a posture of searching, rather than knowing. It demands that we reflect the world as it is, not the world as we may wish it to be. It requires journalists

to be willing to exonerate someone deemed a villain or inter-
rogate someone regarded as a hero. It insists on sharing what
we learn – fully and fairly – regardless of whom it may upset or
what the political consequences might be.

This ethos, he continued, 'tacking as it does against the with-
us-or-against-us certainty of this polarized moment' obviously
'requires a steadfast, sometimes uncomfortable commitment
to journalistic process over personal conviction'.

Sulzberger acknowledged that the *Times* had fallen short
many times, from its early coverage of the Soviet Union to
the lead-up to the Iraq War. He also admitted that detractors
would no doubt seize opportunities to criticize him personally,
including his handling of the Tom Cotton affair. But failures to
live up to an ideal should not be cause for discarding it. In this
polarized era, he stressed, the ethos was in fact 'the exact tonic
the world needs most'.

There is some evidence to suggest that the public agrees. In
their defence of objectivity, in the most recent edition of *The
Elements of Journalism*, Kovach and Rosenstiel write that 'the
data continue to show that declining trust has more to do with
the perception that journalists have failed to live up to those
values'.[26] This has certainly been my experience interacting
with the public, and the experience of many of the journalists
that I have interviewed. 'Just give us the facts', the public tells
us, again and again. In tweets, in online comments sections, in
emails and letters to the editor, in ombudsman complaints, the
public asks us to deliver straight news. Audiences would like
us, to the best of our ability, to gather the facts and the range of
perspectives and to trust people to make up their own minds
about what it all means.

Even objectivity's chief critics will admit that this sentiment
appears to be widespread. Margaret Sullivan shared in her
memoir *Newsroom Confidential* that she'd made a point of
talking to people about their perceptions of the news whenever

she travelled: 'I'd often hear that they wanted less opinion – less spin, as they saw it. They would say something like: "Just give me the facts and let me make up my own mind."' People told her that journalists 'should keep their own point of view out of their work'.[27] Marty Baron said something similar in a 2023 *Washington Post* piece, adapted from a speech at Brandeis University.[28] 'Most in the public, in my experience, expect my profession to be objective', he said. 'Dismissing their expectations – outright defying them – is an act of arrogance.' He continued, 'Most importantly, it fails the cause of truth.'

'I believe our profession would benefit from listening more *to* the public and from talking less *at* the public, as if we knew it all', Baron stressed. 'I believe we should be more impressed with what we don't know than with what we know – or think we know. In journalism, we could use more humility – and less hubris.'

The preference for this approach has been confirmed by anecdotal accounts, by copious amounts of online feedback, by government polls, and by extensive research from the Reuters Institute for the Study of Journalism. Its report, 'The relevance of impartial news in a polarised world',[29] from 2021, demonstrates that audiences place a high value on impartiality, despite the complexity of the notion. Most want to be exposed to a wide range of perspectives and are more concerned about suppressing speech than about the risks of giving airtime to extreme views. All told, the study found 'detailed evidence that impartiality – along with accuracy – remains a bedrock of trust in the news media'.

These findings are complicated by the fact that there's also evidence that news consumers pay more attention to news outlets that confirm their own viewpoints. A recent study from Stanford University researchers[30] expanded this partisan-oriented line of argument, finding that the public often preferences partisan alignment over truth in news, and that this trend in fact occurs across the political and educational spectrums. 'We were a bit surprised to see how widespread this tendency was', the lead author Michael Schwalbe told *Stanford Report*.[31] 'People were engaging in a lot of resistance to inconvenient truths.'

To complicate matters even further, as the Columbia professor Michael Schudson noted in a 2022 paper for the *Daedalus* journal, 'What does "trust in the media" mean?',[32] when it comes to the issue of trust, it 'may even be that people answering a pollster are not trying to report accurately their level of trust but are acting politically to align themselves with their favored party's perceived critique of the media'. In an era as polarized as ours, this is highly plausible, and Schudson has urged media observers not to take poll results at face value but to evaluate them with a healthy scepticism.

Still, as vital as these arguments undoubtedly are, as someone who has received somewhere between hundreds and thousands of emails and social media messages and online comments from the public on this topic, I have to say that the partisan explanation for low trust does not fully track with what I hear from the public. A good portion of the messages that I have received don't neatly conform to partisan narratives. Many people say that they are aware of the tendency to favour their preferred viewpoint, and actively resist that by seeking out news that does not confirm their bias, or that at least complicates a story by acknowledging other viewpoints. Many, too, express deep disillusionment with oversimplified or inaccurate media coverage from their own side, particularly during overheated moments like the pandemic and the racial reckoning. And many share frustrations with media on both sides, reporting how difficult they find it these days to ascertain the facts. Ultimately, in interactions with the public, I cannot escape the impression that most people do not distrust the media for vague, rote reasons but instead for achingly specific ones – indeed, they frequently cite the specific wording in the specific stories that they believe falls short. I am cognizant, too, that the partisan explanation could be seized by media as an excuse to let ourselves off the hook. If news consumers themselves are the problem, we get to avoid doing the difficult but necessary work of examining our own failings.

This returns me to what I see as the chief concern in the objectivity debate: how we have alienated the public that we are meant to serve. In the end, the problem is not solely the message that 'moral clarity' advocates send to an already sceptical public – that the media is no longer even passingly concerned with fairness and fact-finding – but also the reality that privileging morality over truth-seeking reliably produces errors.

It is the media's lack of accuracy, then, that should most concern journalists when thinking through the spiral of lost public trust. Accuracy is, above everything else, the virtue that journalists should most prize. When we get the facts wrong, we fail the public.

6

A Failure to Acknowledge Mistakes

In late 2022, thousands gathered at Roy Thomson Hall, in Toronto, to watch four prominent journalists spar at the prestigious Munk Debates.[1] The resolution: 'Don't trust mainstream media.' Because the semi-annual event holds an audience vote at the beginning and at the end of the evening, attendees that night had the rare experience of watching public trust in the media erode *in real time.* It was an astonishing spectacle, with Matt Taibbi and the British journalist Douglas Murray roundly defeating the *New York Times* columnist Michelle Goldberg and the *New Yorker* writer Malcolm Gladwell.

From where I was sitting that night, the debate was won when Taibbi laid out, in his opening argument for the resolution, his theory of what has gone wrong. The news veteran grew up in a family of journalists, but said he now mourns for the press, because it has destroyed itself 'by getting away from its basic function, which is just to tell us what's happening'. He continued:

> My father had a saying: 'The story's the boss'. In the American context, this means that if the facts tell you the Republicans

were the villains in a political disaster, then you write it that way. If the facts point more to the Democrats, you write that. If they're both culpable, as was often the case for me when I investigated Wall Street for almost ten years after the 2008 crash, you write the story that way. We're not supposed to thumb the scale. Our job is just to call things as we see them and leave the rest up to you. But we don't do that now. The story is no longer the boss. Instead, we sell narrative, in a dys- functional new business model.

Taibbi argued that most audiences of mainstream media outlets, whether on the left or on the right, are now politically homogeneous. And this 'bifurcated system' is 'fundamentally untrustworthy', because it involves selecting which facts to highlight 'based on considerations other than truth or newsworthiness'. The result is not journalism, but rather political entertainment – and thus unreliable.

'With editors now more concerned with retaining audience than getting things right', Taibbi went on, traditional practices have been thrown out. Silent edits have become common, as have anonymous sources. Serious accusations are now levelled without calling subjects for comment. In the Trump era, 'an extraordinary number of "bombshells" went sideways', including multiple allegations made in the 2016 Steele dossier that were repeated in the press. 'A good journalist should always be ashamed of error', Taibbi said, 'and it bothers me to see so many of my colleagues not ashamed'.

James Bennet made a similar point in his *1843* essay about the Tom Cotton affair:

> The *Times* was slow to break it to its readers that there was less to Trump's ties to Russia than they were hoping, and more to Hunter Biden's laptop, that Trump might be right that covid came from a Chinese lab, that masks were not always effective

against the virus, that shutting down schools for many months was a bad idea.

To date, there has been almost no reflection about how we could have gotten so much so wrong. But the fact that we in the press refrain from self-criticism does not stop the public from demanding it of us. The complaints that I see most regularly centre on trends in pandemic coverage, specifically on a lack of proportionality, a negativity bias, a deliberate omission of dissenting voices, and an unwillingness to acknowledge errors. From the moment that the pandemic was first declared, as the former Canadian Broadcasting Corporation radio documentarian David Cayley wrote in the *Literary Review of Canada* magazine in 2020,[2] 'newspapers excluded all other subjects from their pages for weeks on end – as if it were almost indecent to speak of anything else. CBC Radio, with a few exceptions, followed suit. Soon, the pandemic filled the sky.' Was this tsunami of coverage proportional? Or did it instead drum up unhealthy levels of fear, in both the media and the public? Is anyone in leadership going to go back and assess it?

'Media reporting on COVID has been replete with doom, gloom, and hysteria', the Canadian physicians Martha Fulford, J. Edward Les, and Pooya Kazemi pointed out in the *National Post* newspaper in 2022.[3] They cited a report from the US's National Bureau of Economic Research that showed that in major American media outlets, 91 per cent of pandemic stories were negative in tone, compared with 65 per cent of stories in science journals and 54 per cent of articles in major media outside the United States. 'Exaggerating the risk of COVID-19 is harmful', the group warned, 'given the profound negative consequences for children, parents and society. It engenders a perpetual and paralyzing cycle of anxiety and fear, with many unable to return to normalcy.'

I asked Kazemi about that column and others on a Zoom call in 2024. 'There was quite a discrepancy between what I was reading in the medical literature, as well as what was happening in various jurisdictions, especially in Europe, versus what was happening in the North American context and what was being reported in the media', he recalled. He and his colleagues wanted to urge journalists to consult a wider range of experts and present differing views. 'The media was basically feeding one narrative to the population', Kazemi said. 'It allowed the policy makers to push really bad policies without scrutiny.'

It is this lack of dissenting voices, in my experience, that most rankles the public. It's a criticism that applies to the biggest stories of the pandemic era, including lockdowns, school closures, and widespread vaccine mandates tied to travel, dining, events, and employment. These were unprecedented public policies that had massive impacts on people's daily lives, finances, health, and well-being. Dissenting voices certainly existed, including Martin Kulldorff, then at Harvard, and Stanford scholars Jay Bhattacharya (now head of the National Institutes of Health) and John Ioannidis, a professor of medicine, epidemiology, and population health. Opinions contrary to the news headlines, David Cayley wrote in the *Literary Review of Canada*, 'were easily available to those who sought them out, but they made little dent in the emerging consensus'.[4]

The former *New York Times* columnist Joe Nocera and the *Vanity Fair* contributing editor Bethany McLean have written that 'the weight of evidence seems to be with those who say that lockdowns did not save many lives', counting some fifty studies that come to the same conclusion.[5] Nocera told me[6] that one of the main reasons that he and McLean wrote their book *The Big Fail: What the Pandemic Revealed About Who America Protects and Who It Leaves Behind*[7] was because 'nobody else is doing it, and it needs to be done'. Mark Woolhouse, an esteemed British epidemiologist, also told me[8] that the lockdowns were not proportionate, sustainable, or effective. And Princeton professors Frances Lee and Stephen Macedo, authors of *In Covid's Wake: How Our Politics Failed Us*, told me that they found no evidence that non-pharmaceutical interventions reduced mortality.[9] 'The states in the U.S. that were more stringent in their use of non-pharmaceutical interventions, the states that maintained stay-at-home orders longer, the states that kept schools closed longer – there was a significant variation in the U.S. – they did not do significantly better', Lee said. 'In fact, at the end of 2020, the first year where we didn't have a vaccine and where variation in the use of these non-pharmaceutical interventions was quite wide, at the end of that first year, there's just not a difference between the more stringent and the less stringent states in their Covid outcomes, as gauged by mortality'. Given the well-established costs of the lockdowns, detailed in *In Covid's Wake* – including business failures, public debt, unemployment, social dislocation, and compromised physical and mental health – a more robust public debate would clearly have been profoundly useful.

Similarly, despite the muted warnings of dissenting experts in medicine and public health, school closures were allowed to roll out with almost no mainstream media scrutiny. As ProPublica's Alec MacGillis correctly anticipated in his 2020 reporting, these closures were especially devastating for marginalized youth.[10] The *New York Times* has now reported that 'the more time students spent in remote instruction, the further they fell behind', and 'extended closures did little to stop the spread of Covid'.[11] Yet too few media organizations have admitted that they were overly credulous of officials, uncritically accepting closures as the only sensible public policy.

'The notion that the entire response was based on enormously dubious and shaky foundations should be tremendously troubling to everyone', the American journalist David Zweig told me. In his recent book, *An Abundance of Caution: American Schools, the Virus, and a Story of Bad Decisions*,[12] he chronicled his investigation into the decision-making behind the American school closures, which impacted some 50 million children. His reporting revealed modelling based not on a firm foundation of actual data, but on other modelling projections. At the bottom of one such chain he unravelled, he found an arbitrary number, chosen because an actual number could not be found. Zweig's reporting also revealed that the six-foot rule of social distancing that kept many children in hybrid learning models and out of classrooms full-time due to space issues, had no known scientific or medical or epidemiological roots, and no ascertainable factual basis. Zweig told me that he wrote the book because he wanted a record to exist of this flawed decision-making – and of the media's failure to ask basic questions as it unfolded. 'There was this incredibly unearned degree of certainty within which these directives were given to the American public, and there became this just bizarre, almost religious type of adherence to these metrics', he told me.[13] Meanwhile, schools in many parts of Europe were open, with millions of children in class and 'no effect at all that was noticeable'.

In the wake of these extended school closures, Alec MacGillis has reported for *ProPublica* and the *New Yorker*, America now finds itself in the midst of a crisis of school absenteeism.[14] It is highest in the cities, where some cities are above 50 per cent chronically absent students, but it is happening everywhere. 'It's pretty extraordinary', MacGillis told me.[15] 'The rates are even going up in middle-class suburbs.' In some families there has been 'a complete erosion of the norm of going to school'. Such absenteeism, he wrote in 2024, 'underlies much of what has beset young people in recent years, including falling school achievement, deteriorating mental health – exacerbated by social isolation – and elevated youth violence and car thefts, some occurring during school hours'. Confronting the absenteeism crisis, he told me, means reckoning with the decisions that led to the school closures in the first place. 'So much of it did have to do with Donald Trump, and with the extreme, negative polarization that you saw happening in the Trump years and into the pandemic', MacGillis said.

'Trump might be saying a whole bunch of things that are nonsense', Zweig told me. 'But that doesn't mean that the public health authorities didn't spectacularly fail and lie to us, and that the media aided this process.' Trump may have been wrong on a whole lot of things, he continued, but he happened to have been right about schools. 'There was no way that this was acceptable for the enemy, for this odious figure, to be correct on anything', he told me. 'That's how we ended up with an entire elite apparatus within the United States continuing and perpetuating a policy that was manifestly stupid from day one.'

As well as Zweig and MacGillis, former NPR reporter Anya Kamenetz was among the few in the mainstream press to warn about this at the beginning of the pandemic. In her early career, she'd reported on the school closures in the wake of Hurricane Katrina, in her hometown New Orleans, and knew how devastating they would be, particularly for marginalized youth. For such students, school closures meant the loss not just of education but of a safe place, nourishing meals, and contact with caring adults. Her book *The Stolen Year: How COVID Changed Children's Lives, and Where We Go Now*[16] chronicles the ensuing crisis in hunger, physical safety, and emotional well-being, particularly for lower income children, who often had parents working outside the home. 'People could see it', she told me.[17] 'It was almost like it was suppressed evidence, this idea that, yeah, if you close schools, the kids who have the most disadvantages at home are going to suffer the most. That was known from the beginning, and it should have been surfaced constantly whenever we have this conversation about the pros and the cons.'

Turning our attention to my own country, the media here was more conformist than that of the United States, which at least had a conservative press to serve as some kind of counterweight. Here, the majority of the mainstream media is left leaning, with the exception of the *National Post* newspaper, the flagship national paper for the country's largest chain, the *Toronto Sun* newspaper, and morning talk radio (though, emerging from the pandemic era, there has been a number of conservative start-ups). During Covid, narrative conformity tended to be more pronounced here. As a result, vaccine mandates rolled out without any serious press scrutiny, contributing to one of the biggest media mistakes in Canada in recent years. That debacle involved the 2022 Freedom Convoy that saw truckers across the country protest against the mandates and widespread closures, including a caravan that drove across the nation to Ottawa, staging what turned out to be a three-week blockade. But before the truckers had even arrived in the capital, Gary Mason at the *Globe and Mail* newspaper declared that it was 'clear' the demonstration had been 'hijacked by a fringe element that sounds an awful lot like the "freedom fighters" and "patriots" who gathered at the U.S. Capitol building on Jan. 6, 2021, and ended up storming the premises in a poorly organized coup d'etat'.[18] On Twitter, the *Toronto Star* columnist Bruce Arthur later described protesters as a 'home grown hate farm'.[19] A former *CBC News* anchor in Ottawa, Lucy van Oldenbarneveld, referred to the truckers as a 'feral mob'.[20]

Ultimately, however, the Public Order Emergency Commission (POEC) told a different story. POEC reviewed 85,000 documents, interviewed 139 individuals – including then Prime Minister Justin Trudeau – and heard testimony from fifty experts and seventy-six witnesses. In his report concluding that the legal threshold for invoking emergency powers was met, Justice Paul Rouleau noted that while the truckers may have been spreaders of misinformation, they were also victims of it, with false, discrediting reports about the Convoy often amplified – including an attempted apartment building arson that was associated with protesters, which police later confirmed had no connection to demonstrators.[21] Justice Rouleau also acknowledged the existence of 'unfair generalizations from some public officials that suggested all protesters were extremists'. Canada's Federal Court later contradicted the conclusion of that commission, deeming the government's invocation of the Emergencies Act illegal, and the resulting regulations, including the freezing of protesters' bank accounts, a violation of the Canadian Charter of Rights and Freedoms. Justice Mosley concluded that 'there was no national emergency justifying the invocation of the *Emergencies Act* and the decision to do so was therefore unreasonable and *ultra vires*'.[22] (The ruling was subsequently upheld by the Federal Court of Appeal.)

The protest in Ottawa was largely portrayed in the media as far right, extremist, and driven by foreign funders. But in the end, it turned out to be overwhelmingly non-violent, with no weapons recovered and no serious injuries sustained, drawing the majority of its financial support from within the country[23]. (Weapons were seized, however, at a solidarity blockade at the border in Coutts, Alberta, and several men were eventually found guilty of mischief and firearm offences though not guilty of the far more serious charge of conspiracy to murder police.) Ultimately, while the Ottawa blockade was no doubt highly disruptive, and acutely so for the city's downtown residents, the Royal Canadian Mounted Police (RCMP) and the Canadian Intelligence Security Service (CSIS) testified at POEC that it posed no national security threat. After lengthy trials, its two main organizers, Tamara Lich and Chris Barber, were only convicted of mischief and counselling others to commit mischief, and handed eighteen-month conditional sentences that included twelve months of home arrest and six months under curfew. As the *Wall Street Journal* editorial board pointed out, neither had criminal records, and the court acknowledged that they had had good intentions and had repeatedly urged protesters to remain peaceful.[24]

I asked the Lakehead University professor and constitutional law expert Ryan Alford, who had standing at the POEC, about the disconnect between the reality at the protests and the press's portrayal of the truckers. He observed that members of law enforcement, who ran intelligence operations on the ground, testified 'how this was not being driven by those ideologically motived extremists who, if they existed, had only the most tangential connection to what was going on, particularly in Ottawa'.[25]

In addition to a lack of press scrutiny around the security threat the protest posed, there was also a lack of questioning when it came to the class conflict underlying tensions, which went largely unexamined in the mainstream press. Much of the media reaction to the truckers was hyperbolic, speculative, and driven by fear of a perceived 'other'. (For example, the *Canadian Press* headline: 'Calling Ottawa protests "peaceful" downplays non-violent dangers, critics say'.[26]) There was an aspect of class condescension, a lot of it seemingly unconscious, that was evident. Much was made in the media of how uncouth the protesters were, with their loud honking, odorous fumes, lack of masks, foul language, and unmistakably blue-collar affect. 'It was like being at a truck stop all day', one local church employee complained to the CBC.[27] The coverage was epitomized, the retired CBC broadcaster David Cayley told me,[28] by an episode of the CBC show, *The Fifth Estate*,[29] 'in which the whole thing was treated entirely as a problem – a problem of public safety, a problem of order, a problem of noise and inconvenience'.

There was a feeling among the press corps that the story was uniquely distasteful, and that any alternative conclusions about the truckers were basically boorish. This dynamic was ultimately self-reinforcing. Those outside the media may not comprehend how subtle and insidious such a dynamic can be in enforcing ideological uniformity; as *Tablet*'s Jacob Siegel has said on a podcast, 'more often than not, it's that the person who is being pressured has already fully internalized the idea that to report on the wrong kind of story, to say the wrong kind of thing, would simply be gauche'.[30] He added: 'To be gauche in that way is essentially unforgiveable . . . It's to step outside of the bounds of civilized society.'

With some notable exceptions, including Rupa Subramanya, a then *National Post* columnist who wrote a viral piece for *The Free Press*,[31] many Canadian journalists were reluctant to interact with the truckers at all. This lack of contact allowed fears to fester. The class dynamic proved particularly incendiary given the fact that pandemic policies had already widened the gap between knowledge workers – who, the Liberal member of parliament Joël Lightbound memorably pointed out,[32] 'could earn a living on a Macbook at the cottage' – and working-class Canadians, who experienced the crisis very differently.

The chasm between reporters and the people they cover predictably has a negative impact on the quality of coverage, and on public trust. But it also has a more subtle and more insidious effect: it discourages journalists from challenging those in power. And this, in turn, leads to further failures.

7

A Failure to Insulate the
Media from Power

By the time the pandemic hit, as we have seen, the press had become far more ideologically homogeneous – highly educated, progressive, from economically privileged backgrounds, concentrated in major cities, having little contact with other perspectives, and increasingly anxious about their ability to realize the lives towards which they'd long worked. But the media had, as the journalist David Zweig told me, also coalesced around a certain way of approaching work and career that proved to be a liability. 'The type of person who's working at the *New York Times* got straight As in high school, then they went to Brown, then maybe they went to Columbia for journalism school', he told me on my podcast in 2025.[1] 'The way they got there was not by being an independent thinker, generally.' This by no means described everyone, he stressed. There were lots of excellent reporters at the *Times* and at other top media – but 'you don't get there by being an iconoclast'. It's not surprising then, he said, that these were not the people asking the questions that could lead to 'very uncomfortable and inconvenient truths that might support the enemy on the other side'.

Nowhere was this dynamic more evident than in the coverage of President Biden's failing health.

For months, the White House was adamant that the president was fit for office, and the mainstream media largely repeated this position. The *Washington Post*'s Jonathan Capehart dismissed the topic out of hand, telling PBS: 'We've spent way too much time talking about this president's age.'[2] As evidence to the contrary gained steam in the independent press, legacy outlets continued to resist, with the *New York Times* going so far as to describe legitimate, if unflatteringly edited video clips of the American leader as misleading 'cheap fakes'.[3] The notable exception was the *Wall Street Journal*, which published a bombshell investigation from Annie Linskey and Siobhan Hughes in early June of 2024.[4] The Poynter Institute's Tom Jones responded by writing that 'tales suggesting Biden's decline are flimsy, at best',[5] and at *Media Matters*, Matt Gertz argued that the story was 'comically weak'. As Fox News noted,[6] Jake Tapper said on air that the piece was 'mostly based on observations of Republicans', while MSNBC's Joe Scarborough called it a 'Trump hit piece on Biden'. The *Washington Post*'s Jennifer Rubin, meanwhile, opined that the 'shoddy' article was 'essentially the promotion of a right-wing meme'.[7] CNN's media reporter at the time, Oliver Darcy, wrote that the story had 'glaring problems' and that the paper owed 'its readers – *and the public* – better'.[8]

Such commentary ended abruptly after the president's catastrophic presidential debate in late June, when the American public was able to see for themselves the state of decline that Biden was experiencing. The *Journal*'s editor Emma Tucker told *Semafor*[9] that her reporters 'took a lot of grief for covering a story that needed to be covered and that no other mainstream publishers were willing to touch', that she was proud of them, and that she felt vindicated – 'very much so'. Starting with reporting from Olivia Nuzzi in *New York Magazine*[10] – where she was later fired, after revelations of an emotional affair with 2024 presidential candidate Robert F. Kennedy Jr. – and culminating in Jake Tapper and Alex Thompson's book,

Original Sin: President Biden's Decline, Its Cover-Up, and His Disastrous Choice to Run Again,[11] a picture has emerged of a fourth estate that had failed to adequately challenge power. Speaking to Megyn Kelly,[12] Tapper said that the press had not been critical enough – and, to Tapper's credit, he included himself in that group. 'I think that we need to be sceptical of everything that we are told by people in power', he later said on PBS's *Washington Week* show.[13] 'That obviously should be the mantra of being a journalist to begin with.' He added: 'Politicians lie. White Houses lie. Power is an aphrodisiac. And we just need to all remember that and not take at face value anything that we're told.'

Like other failures during the pandemic, it appears that the press's errors regarding Biden's health resulted from groupthink and misplaced ideological certainty. Given that fears about Trump were widespread, the press was hesitant to challenge the White House's narrative or consider anything that might assist Republicans in retaking the presidency in 2024.

What's striking is that this conformity and timidity from the press corps occurred in the United States, where the media does not receive government funding (with the exception, at least until recently, of NPR and PBS), and thus cannot be accused of having a direct relationship with government, or of relying on it for survival. In Canada, this has not been the case.

Indeed, during this extreme moment in history – rife with all of the challenges that I have outlined – the federal government, arguably at the behest of powerful lobbyists for the News Media Canada trade organization, was busy attempting to rescue Canadian journalism. Ottawa's subsidies, which included a $595-million bailout, were meant to be temporary but have since been extended and expanded, now covering a significant portion of journalists' salaries. So far, these measures have failed to stem cutbacks and closures. As the Ottawa-based outlet *Blacklock's Reporter* noted in a brief[14] to parliament's Standing Committee on Canadian Heritage, the *Winnipeg Free Press* newspaper took $822,000 in annual payroll rebates before shutting its Parliament Hill bureau in 2023; the *Toronto Star* newspaper qualified for $6 million in annual rebates but nevertheless closed its Vancouver office in 2023 and cut 600 Metroland Media jobs. And the SaltWire newspaper chain in Atlantic Canada, which accepted subsidies, filed for creditor protection.[15]

Not only have the subsidies failed to stem outlet closures and cuts, *Blacklock's* has reported, they have also negatively impacted the media's relationship with the public.[16] In its polling weeks before newsroom payroll rebates were increased, Canada's Privy Council – an advisory body to the government – found the public opposed the media bailout. Few respondents agreed that supporting the Canadian news industry should be a priority.

A segment of the public now regularly espouses the idea that the Canadian media is a 'mouthpiece' for the Prime Minister's Office, an accusation that Lana Payne, national president for Unifor, Canada's largest private sector union, has said her members in the media now face.[17] It's a criticism all too familiar to many journalists. 'The first thing any idiot on Twitter says is, "Oh, I guess you're waiting for your paycheque from the government"', the *Globe and Mail* newspaper columnist Andrew Coyne told me.[18] 'Now obviously, that's loony and cheap. But it feeds that perception – and to some extent it's a reality.' Marc Edge, a media columnist for the website *Canadian Dimension*, agreed: 'I think a lot of people look at [the subsidies] and see the press as being on the payroll of the federal government. I don't think that's quite true. I don't think most journalists consider themselves on the payroll of the federal government. But this is a public perception. And, in many cases, perception is reality.'[19]

Journalism derives its credibility from its independence. Failing to insulate itself from the power it is supposed to hold to account was always a terrible idea – but it's an especially terrible idea right now. Certainly, the public seems to think so: an Angus Reid poll in July 2023 found that a majority of Canadians – 59 per cent – opposed the government funding private newsrooms.[20] (Canada's example, it must be said, offers a stark reminder for American proponents of government media funding to think critically about the potential drawbacks of this model.)

This destructive dynamic was highlighted in Canada's recent federal election, which saw the media itself become an issue. On the one side, the Conservative candidate Pierre Poilievre promised to significantly defund the national public broadcaster, the Canadian Broadcasting Corporation, and criticized government subsidies for privately owned newsrooms (though he later expressed support for subsidies supporting local journalism). On the other side, Liberal candidate Mark Carney said he'd increase CBC's funding by $150 million – adding to its roughly $1.4 billion-dollar annual budget – and maintain the subsidy regime for private newsrooms. The press, almost entirely subsidized by the incumbent Liberal government, saw every move scrutinized by a public who reminded them, daily, who was paying their bills.

Trading objectivity for activism left the media open to ideological capture. It stifled critical thinking. It paved the way for mistakes, which resulted in both lost audiences and trust. It also, in Canada, put the media in the position of accepting government money despite the risk of further jeopardizing public trust. And now, with Trump's radical new presidency threatening to kick off a fresh new trust spiral, journalists on both sides of the border face a choice: do we do what we have done for the past eight years – hemorrhaging trust, audience numbers, and revenue – or do we correct course and get back to the basics, most especially the aim of objectivity?

8

A Fork in the Road

The public radio show *On the Media* made its own decision in its 2024 election coverage, when it circled back to the questions it raised on that fateful morning in 2016 that I opened this book with. Donald Trump was up in the polls again, and the program finally had to concede that he wasn't going away.

The same couldn't be said for co-host Bob Garfield, who had been fired in the great media purges. His co-host and de facto boss, Brooke Gladstone, had announced his departure on air in 2021: 'Bob Garfield is out this week, and as many of you know by now, every week, having been fired after a warning and other efforts at amelioration for a pattern of bullying behaviour. The entire staff agreed with that decision.'[1] (Garfield later wrote on Substack that one incident involved him telling a producer that he was 'sick and tired of being told how woke I'm not'.[2])

Despite all that had changed at *On the Media*, the central question had not. 'He has never paid a price for his bare-faced lies', Gladstone declared of the once and future president on its 2023 year-end program[3]. 'He challenges journalistic conventions of polite interrogation with pyrotechnical defiance. But to such an irreconcilable electorate, how should the media cover Trump in 2024?' Suggestions from guests on the show constituted a buffet of the same old solutions, including being less squeamish about using words like 'fascism' to describe Trump's political movement and working harder to stress the colossal stakes of the election to listeners.

While the sky was yet again falling at *On the Media*, cooler heads prevailed elsewhere. Consider a forum at Stony Brook University's School of Communication and Journalism in Long Island, New York.[4] Hosted by the SBU professor Musa al-Gharbi, it brought together the *Vox* co-founder and now Substacker Matt Yglesias, the *New York Times* opinion writer Jane Coaston, and James Bennet, the former *New York Times* opinion editor, to talk through strategies for the coming year. Yglesias, in particular, focused on turning the temperature down on Trump alarmism and scaling back on disproportionate volumes of coverage, which, as al-Gharbi pointed out, had already surpassed coverage of any other president in history. (Excluding 'and', 'but', 'the', and other non-substantive terms, 'Trump' was the fourth most used word in the *Times* in 2018, spanning all sections, from sports to fashion.) Trump's four years in office had felt extremely consequential to those covering them, Yglesias reflected, but the best way to handle Trump's excesses, he maintained, was by calmly and painstakingly interrogating them. In other words, by doing journalism.

As for the trust question, Yglesias acknowledged that those who don't trust the media basically have an accurate perception of legacy institutions, such as CNN and the Gray Lady – which is that most staffers are on the left. The people who covered politics at mainstream institutions, he continued, tended to be careful, in order to maintain professional relationships. But the people who covered, say, entertainment, often felt free to indulge in opinion. 'I got to a point, though, working at larger places, where I was constantly being annoyed by random asides that were occurring in articles that weren't really political', Yglesias said. 'I was like, "Don't you guys see? It just discredits us if our review of a Marvel movie is just, in the third paragraph, 'also Donald Trump is bad'".' Nobody read something like that and changed their vote, he said. Instead, they thought, 'this is not a publication whose output I need to take seriously'. News managers were increasingly contemplating that very problem, he said.

Several months later, Joe Kahn, the editor of the *New York Times*, said as much to Ben Smith's start-up outlet, *Semafor*,[5] signalling the paper's attempt to steer itself back to pre-Trump standards. He pushed back on the activist ethos, admitted that the paper had gone 'too far', and said it was now re-establishing norms after these 'excesses'. Turning his attention to ongoing campus protests, and the ethos of some young journalists entering newsrooms, he said: 'The newsroom is not a safe space. It's a space where you're being exposed to lots of journalism, some of which you are not going to like.'

The *Pod Save America* host Dan Pfeiffer, a former Obama aide, had recently complained on Substack that the paper was 'often too worried about seeming balanced to truly articulate the dangers of Trump' and that *Times* journalists 'do not see their job as saving democracy or stopping an authoritarian from taking power'.[6] But Kahn plainly disagreed: 'To say that the threats of democracy are so great that the media is going to abandon its central role as a source of impartial information to help people vote – that's essentially saying that the news media should become a propaganda arm for a single candidate, because we prefer that candidate's agenda.'

'There's a very good chance', he added, 'based on our polling and other independent polling, that [Trump] will win that election in a popular vote. So there are people out there in the world who may decide, based on their democratic rights, to elect Donald Trump as president. It is not the job of the news media to prevent that from happening.'

9

The Future of News

That political prediction was of course, borne out in November of 2024. Donald Trump won the presidency, capturing not just the popular vote but the House and the Senate, and, supported by media and tech billionaires, swiftly enacted an aggressive and controversial agenda, triggering a fresh round of debates about how to cover him and his supporters. Writing in the *Guardian*, Rebecca Solnit captured the prevailing mood (and class condescension) in some parts of the media: 'our mistake was to think we lived in a better country than we do'.[1]

The story documented in these pages is by no means resolved; it continues to unfold, with developments dominating the daily news cycle.

Donald Trump has ratcheted up his rhetoric against the press, insulting the *Washington Post*'s Eugene Robinson as 'incompetent' and calling for his firing after Robinson criticized Republicans for not standing up to Trump.[2] The State Department also paused 'non-mission critical' subscriptions to news organizations around the globe,[3] and the White House banned the Associated Press from events for failing to use Trump's preferred term, the Gulf of America.[4] (A federal judge later ordered their access be restored.[5]) The Pentagon indicated it would rotate NBC News, NPR, the *New York Times*, and *Politico* out of offices,[6] and, in the fall of 2025, issued a memo restricting journalists from reporting any information not 'approved for public release'.[7] The White House has also granted increased access to influencers and podcasters that are friendly to the administration.[8] As this book goes to press, Trump is currently suing several outlets over coverage, including the *Wall Street Journal* and the *New York Times*, and has settled a lawsuit with ABC News. The organization Reporters Without Borders had described press freedom in the United States as 'under siege'.[9]

The radicalism of Trump's second presidency has led many commentators who once critiqued illiberalism on the left to now focus on illiberalism on the right. Concerns about the 'woke right' – a phrase used by the likes of the British podcaster Konstantin Kisin and the American commentator James Lindsay – are now taking centre stage in the discourse. The conservative American author Rod Dreher recently penned an essay for *The Free Press* warning about the threats coming from the radical right.[10] Speaking to its editor Bari Weiss (now the editor-in-chief of CBS News) on a live-stream, he emphasized that liberalism was being fundamentally challenged.[11] The woke left, he said, abandoned classical liberal values in favour of identity politics and tribalism, and now the woke right was doing the same. 'I think that's fundamentally corrupt', he told Weiss.

The British broadcaster Andrew Doyle also warned about this in his recent book, *The End of Woke: How the Culture War Went Too Far and What to Expect from the Counter-Revolution*.[12] A long-time critic of leftist illiberalism, Doyle told me that he sees similar tendencies emerging on the right, including authoritarianism, a preoccupation with group identity, a politics of resentment, calls for censorship, a denial of truth, a disdain for the West, anti-Semitism, and an obsession with moral purity.[13] 'I think it's incontestable that those trends are increasing', he said. 'I can see it all the time. When people complain about the term, they're upset because they associate wokeness with left-wing . . . I reject that premise.'

Certainly, such trends are deeply concerning, and the rise of authoritarian impulses, wherever they originate on the political spectrum, should ring alarms for anyone who wants to see our pluralistic, liberal democracies survive. There are those now who make the argument that Trump presents a threat on par with, if not Hitler, at least elected autocrats elsewhere in the world. This argument should be taken seriously. But it should not grant us licence to abandon our governing principles and practices. For journalists, the solution to extremist threats on either side of the aisle – as well as the temptation towards reactionary responses to them – has been and remains *basic liberalism*. The solution, then, is a renewed commitment to the liberal principles that underpin objectivity, the pursuit of truth, and indeed the entire democratic project.

Journalists who have lived and worked in non-democratic countries drive this point home. Victor Febres, an Atlanta-based journalist originally from Venezuela, stressed to me that it is ultimately not helpful when journalists become activists, no matter how endangered democracy is.[14] In his own country, he said, in the era of Hugo Chavez, establishment media took on a political role. 'They thought that they were the spearhead of the opposition, and they behaved like that', he told me. 'In reality, they were a faction power. They built an agenda, and in that process, they walked over the work of ethical journalists.' Big media ultimately spurred on the damaging dynamics of polarization, with truth-seeking journalists stuck between the extremes on either side, struggling to perform their jobs.

Despite such warnings from international journalists, as fears about Trump's authoritarian impulses mount, it is as yet unclear which way the media in the United States will go. The UK-based veteran war reporter Christiane Amanpour, for instance, said on her podcast that she was so scared to travel to Harvard to give a speech that she carried a burner phone and took other precautions 'as if I was going to North Korea'.[15] Such anxieties were also elevated in an ominous opinion video for the *New York Times*, featuring three experts on fascism.[16] They were so afraid of Trump, they said, they were leaving Yale to join the University of Toronto, comparing their exit to the exodus of German intellectuals in 1930s Germany. One of them, the celebrated author Tim Snyder, had left Yale almost a year prior, and had earlier insisted in print that 'I did not leave Yale because of anything Trump is doing . . . I was not and am not fleeing anything'.[17] A second academic, his wife Marci Shore, told Jane Coaston on her podcast that she was 'a neurotic catastrophist by nature' and that the day Trump was elected she vomited, lying on the floor of her office, barely able to pull herself together to make it to class.[18] The third professor, Jason Stanley, had previously stressed to media that while he was very concerned about Trump, he was also excited about joining the University of Toronto's Munk School of Global Affairs and Public Policy, which was building a prestigious centre for the defence of democracy. The story, then, was more complicated than presented in the *Times* and elsewhere.

In addition to the very real possibility that this kind of coverage could help fuel another panic, it's also increasingly clear that the underlying conditions that keep us susceptible to such intemperance – the media's enduring financial woes – are far from resolved. We have yet to find a workable twenty-first-century business model that will provide the next generation of journalists with stable employment. It should not surprise us, then, that the purges continue, with the latest seeing Sewell Chan ousted from his editorship of the *Columbia Journalism Review* amid staff complaints. For his part, Chan described these complaints on social media as 'normal workplace interactions', and added: 'In a precarious and declining news industry that has lost economic, political, social and even moral capital, the only thing I have as a journalist is my reputation. I intend to defend it.'[19] (In a more disturbing incident, the *CJR* published reporting on sexual misconduct allegations against Wesley Lowery.)

All incentives point to a renewed panic, kicking off a fresh downward spiral in trust – which we obviously cannot afford. This all makes the need for the grounding ethic of objectivity more necessary than ever. In times this chaotic, some stability can be found in its guiding ethos of public service – and its orientation towards curiosity, humility, fairness, and thoroughness, coupled with, crucially, a sincere and sustained attempt to remain politically neutral.

It's a point that was well made by *Times* publisher A.G. Sulzberger in a recent talk at the Kellogg Institute at the University of Notre Dame's Keough School of Global Affairs.[20] Outlining the president's worrying rhetorical and legal attacks, he stressed that a strong, independent, and free press is essential to democracy – and that is more true in our troubled era, not less. The way to maintain press freedom is to renew our commitment to core principles. 'I believe our job is to cover political debates, not to join them', he said. 'We're not the resistance. We are nobody's opposition. We're also nobody's cheerleader. Our loyalty is to the truth and to a public that deserves to know it.'

'Holding fast to our independence in the face of intimidation is not appeasement or acquiescence, as some would suggest', he continued. 'It's certainly not a form of complicity. It's a refusal to allow ourselves to be pressured by anyone into distorting our mission to follow the facts and bring the public the full story.'

While Trump was, in Sulzberger's estimation, following an authoritarian playbook seen elsewhere in the world – cultivating mistrust in media, launching civil suits, using regulatory authority to punish media, encouraging wealthy allies to denigrate the press, and providing increased access to friendly media outlets – he, too, noted that journalists who've

faced government pressure caution us not to allow ourselves to
be baited into behaving like activists. The Hungarian investigative journalist András Pethő, Sulzberger noted, has advised
that 'nothing makes autocrats happier than reporters who por-
tray themselves as crusaders against the regime – or victims
of it'. Journalists with partisan aims are easy to dismiss. They
are, as we've seen throughout this short book, fundamentally
unpopular with the public, which distrusts those with agendas.
As Pethő himself has said: 'If you act like an advocate, you
should not be surprised if you become viewed as such.'[21]

The *Times* has made clear that it will stay focused on the
public interest, maintain its rigorous reporting practices, and
stick to the aim of objective reporting. And, Sulzberger said, if
conditions continued to decline, it will take hope from its long
history, and practical guidance from its experience reporting
in tough conditions elsewhere in the world. There is much
to criticize about the paper's actions during the period I have
written about here; no doubt its coverage, which is vast and
varied, and produced under tight deadlines, frequently falls
short of its own ideals. But in this steadfast commitment to
objectivity, it points the way forward for us all.

Indeed, in the wake of *Washington Post* owner Jeff Bezos's
edict that the paper's opinion section would only publish
pieces in favour of personal liberties and free markets, there's
been a renewed appreciation among the press corps for the
old norms of viewpoint diversity, open debate, and balanced
coverage – and a belated recognition of how the erosion of
these norms has hurt us all. News organizations have begun,
again, to discipline news journalists for partisan social media
posts, with ABC News firing correspondent Terry Moran for
a tweet that labelled Trump a 'world-class hater' and one of
his officials, Stephen Miller, a man 'richly endowed with the
capacity for hatred'.[22]

The encouraging news is that, on the ground level, many of
the journalists that I interviewed while writing this book are

already hard at work cultivating strategies to uphold fairness, resist political polarization, and reorient towards public service. Amanda Ripley has penned a landmark piece, 'Complicating the narratives', with Solutions Journalism, offering multiple practical suggestions to 'revive complexity in a time of false simplicity'.[23] These techniques include conversational and listening skills that seek to unearth the 'understory', or people's personal histories, emotions, contradictions, and motivations.

Polarization induces distress in both us and our audiences, Ripley explained in the essay, and we seek to relieve this discomfort through narrative cohesion. 'Tidy narratives succumb to this urge to simplify, gently warping reality until one side looks good and the other looks evil', she wrote. 'We soothe ourselves with the knowledge that all Republicans are racist rednecks – or all Democrats are precious snowflakes who hate America. Complexity counters this craving, restoring the cracks and inconsistencies that had been air-brushed out of the picture. It's less comforting, yes. But it's also more interesting – and true.' Solutions Journalism has transformed the essay into a training workshop for journalists, and now, through her organization Good Conflict, Ripley is offering the framework to other institutions and individuals grappling with polarization and high conflict.

Ripley is not alone in experimenting with creative solutions to the problems we face. Ross Barkan, a columnist at *New York Magazine*, told me that he's intentionally cultivated a social group outside of 'the confines of the media' so he doesn't have to worry about offending friends when writing against the grain.[24] The *Washington Post*'s Ruby Cramer told me that she has made an effort to step away from social media.[25] For his part, Alec MacGillis of ProPublica works to get out and report from across the country. 'The media has become very concentrated in certain places in America', he told me on my podcast *Lean Out*.[26] 'With that concentration comes the risk of a bubble mindset and groupthink – when you don't even realize that you're missing things because you're all just talking to each other.' This need to venture further afield was echoed, too, by NBC's Vicky Nguyen, who told me it had been illuminating for her to live and work in both red and blue places.[27] 'I've been in border states, and I've been in states where religion and gun rights are very important', she told me. 'I've lived in states where reproductive rights are very important.'

'I'm grateful that as a journalist, I get to ask those questions, in a non-offensive "Oh, it's just my job, I'm curious" [way]', she said. 'I get to have those conversations. Because I think if you're seeking understanding, that's a great goal to have out of any conversation.'

This all brings us to a central question raised in *The Elements of Journalism*: what is journalism for? Is it to gather all the available facts and perspectives, and, to the best of our ability, to relay that to the public so that it may fully participate in the democratic process? Or is it to steer public opinion? Is journalism, at heart, about informing the public – or is it about influencing it? Having read this far, it should come as no surprise that I see our job as one of reflecting the reality around us, in all its messy complexity, and allowing the public to come to its own conclusions.

Given the press's often adversarial role in society, and its mandate to uncover inconvenient truths, we journalists should not expect to be liked, and likely won't be, particularly when it comes to the wealthy and powerful. But, as the former *Times* staffer Andy Mills once pointed out to me, there is a world of difference between being disliked and being fundamentally distrusted.

We should also understand, as Columbia professor Michael Schudson has argued, that a certain level of scepticism of us and our work is healthy and is evidence of a citizenry that is engaged in critical thinking about its institutions, including its fourth estate. We should resist, too, the tendency to romanticize past eras of journalism; one study Schudson cited in his 2022

Daedalus paper, which compared news coverage in ten daily city papers in the early 1960s to that of the same papers in the late 1990s, found newspapers surveyed in the earlier era to be 'naively trusting of government, shamelessly boosterish, unembarrassedly hokey and obliging'. The drop in public trust in all institutions, including the media, Schudson argued, 'was a decline from what was arguably much too unquestioning a level of trust'.

Still, as I hope I have demonstrated here, the press, in recent years, has been guilty of a myopia that's rendered us worthy of heightened scepticism and has lost us excessive amounts of public trust. In the Trump era, we ultimately became too self-absorbed. Under constant financial stress, we allowed ourselves to become overly focused on our own struggles, our own internal battles, and our own political convictions. Ultimately, that resulted in us becoming captive to our own limited perspectives. Going forward, we need to expand our focus out to include all those that we are meant to serve.

This starts with listening to the public. This is what democracy, in fact, is all about. If we believe in democracy, we must believe in the public. And what the public is telling us boils down to this: stop indulging in moral panics. Stop ignoring dissenting views. Stop letting your personal politics blind you to the facts, making you vulnerable to mistakes. Stop inserting your views into the news. Admit mistakes when you do make them. Many of the problems facing us are multifaceted and difficult to solve. But the answer to our trust problem is right in front of us. The answer is with the public we serve.

Afterword

I am, of course, not just a passive observer of the media, but an active participant – and one who has spent my entire adult life steeped in its struggles. This project is not just based on extensive research and reporting, then. It is also informed by my own experiences, working in print, digital, TV, radio, and podcasts, for outlets in the United States and in Canada, in legacy media and now in the independent press. I have loved it all, in spite of its many challenges.

I have not just watched the media developments that I have written about here but have lived them. They have been the air I breathed, ever since I first stumbled on a minor news scoop as a reporter in the student press in the summer of 2001, on a story about a Hong Kong Christian Association report on Disney contractors and sweatshop labour, obtaining comment from Disney. A local independent newsweekly in Vancouver, B.C. picked up my story, kickstarting my career. In my early years, I worked as a music journalist for that newspaper and then wound up an online columnist at a prominent New York hip-hop magazine at the height of the snark blog era. I moved on to become a writer and then editor at a Toronto women's magazine right before the recession hit (but even then, my first week on the job saw a round of lay-offs). That job allowed me a small taste of magazines' golden era, so poignantly captured in Graydon Carter's recent memoir, *When the Going Was Good: An Editor's Adventures During the Last Golden Age of Magazines*,[1] before the collapse came, and the glitzy parties and celebrity photo shoots dried up.

In 2013, I took a role as an interview producer at a popular TV talk show at the national public broadcaster in Canada. There, at the Canadian Broadcasting Corporation, I discovered my true love, current affairs radio, moving on to work on about a dozen radio shows, in both Toronto and Vancouver, in a number of rank-and-file producer roles. (All the while, I freelanced for numerous newspapers and magazines and websites.) I was at CBC Radio throughout the first two years of the pandemic and through the Great Awokening I have recounted here, becoming increasingly baffled by the explosion of identity politics, the erosion of journalistic norms, and the stifling of newsroom debate, particularly in the aftermath of the Wendy Mesley scandal.

Like so many of the journalists I've interviewed, the culture wars eventually came for me. I too was caught up in the newsroom revolts of the era, eventually ending my contract a year early and taking the leap to Substack in early 2022, where I wrote about my reasons for leaving the CBC. The post went viral, and I too was the subject of an online pile-on that left me with many questions about where we in the media had gone wrong – and where we should all go from here.

When the dust settled, I set out to explore such questions, conducting interviews on more than 200 episodes of my current affairs podcast, *Lean Out with Tara Henley,* trying to make sense of the moment that we were all living through. My hope is that, as the political winds have now changed again and the media is once again reeling, as destabilized as ever, this book helps us think through, and debate, some answers.

Acknowledgements

All books are collaborative endeavours, but this one uniquely so. *The Trust Spiral* would not exist without Kyle Wyatt, editor-in-chief of the *Literary Review of Canada*, who invited me to write the 2024 Massey Essay on the state of media, on which this book is based. Kyle is an old-school editor in the very best sense: Smart, skilled, and uncommonly brave. I am grateful for his editorial instincts, for conversations over lunch, and for his painstaking work getting the essay to press. Thanks, as well, to Kyle's fantastic team at the magazine, especially Barbara Czarnecki, Caroline Noël, Emily Mernin, David Venn, and illustrator Karsten Petrat. The Massey Essay is a partnership between the *Literary Review of Canada* and Massey College, a University of Toronto community dedicated to open inquiry that I'm proud to belong to. Many thanks to Massey College, especially Emily Mockler and Jonathan Rose for *The Trust Spiral*'s public forum, at which I was fortunate to be joined by interlocutor Rudyard Griffiths of The Munk Debates and The Hub. Appreciation also goes to the National Magazine Awards in Canada, for recognizing *The Trust Spiral* as a finalist.

I have been delighted to get the opportunity to work with Polity's brilliant publisher Ian Malcolm. I am honoured that he saw a book in this essay and am grateful for his insights and queries, all of which immeasurably improved the manuscript. I have long admired Ian's work and am thrilled to become a member of Polity's thriving intellectual community. I owe much to all of the wonderful Polity staff who worked tirelessly to get this book into shape and out into the world, including assistant editor Olivia Jackson, production head Neil de Cort, copy editor Phil Dines, and publicity head Breffni O'Connor. Thanks, too, to David A. Gee for an arresting cover design.

Much appreciation, as always, to my stellar – and steadfast – agents Chris Casuccio and John Pearce at Westwood Creative Artists for their support and guidance.

Gratitude goes to all of the guests that I have interviewed in five years of hosting the *Lean Out* podcast, who have helped shape my understanding of what's happening with our media. Thanks to the *National Review* and Sebastian Junger for permission to include the epigraph. And thank you as well to the fellow journalists, authors, podcasters, and academics, whose work I admire and who graciously took time out of their busy lives to blurb this book, including Thomas Chatterton Williams, Eric Kaufmann, Ruy Teixeira, William Deresiewicz, Uri Berliner and Meghan Daum. Your support means a lot. I am also grateful to Massey College Journalism Fellow Jordan Michael Smith, who read the early draft of the manuscript with an informed and critical eye.

Many thanks, as well, to the four blind review readers on this project, who generously shared their time and expertise; their feedback was absolutely invaluable. Any errors that remain are of course my own.

I would like to extend thanks, too, to the next generation of journalists that worked with me on my podcast during the period that I researched this book, including Harrison Lowman, Luke Ettinger, and Lauren Toffan, as well as guest host Aaron Pete. Thanks as well to my co-hosts at the Full Press media criticism podcast, Harrison Lowman and Peter

Menzies, and The Hub for seeing the need for a Canadian media criticism show.

Thank you to Hamish McKenzie, Chris Best, and Sophia Efthimiatou at Substack, the platform where much of my reporting here first appeared. It provided me with the editorial freedom to do this work, and I am beyond grateful. Big gratitude to *Lean Out*'s readers and listeners in more than 150 countries, and to the subscribers who generously fund my work. I can't thank you enough.

On a personal note, this book would not have been possible without the support of my husband and our family and friends across Canada and in Louisiana. The stress of the news cycle was frequently offset by conversations and cooking – and, when I was lucky, coffee and King cake.

Notes

Prologue

1 Junger, S. (2024) 'When journalism dies', *National Review*, 25 January. Available at: https://www.nationalreview.com/magazine /2024/03/when-journalism-dies/. Used with permission.

2 On the Media (2016) 'Now what?' *WNYC Studios*. Available at: https://www.wnycstudios.org/podcasts/otm/episodes/now-what.

3 Brenan, M. (2025) 'Trust in Media at New Low of 28% in U.S.', *Gallup.com*. Available at: https://news.gallup.com/poll/695762/tr ust-media-new-low.aspx.

4 Semafor Events (2025) 'Innovating to restore trust in news: A nationalsummit', *Semafor*. Available at: https://www.semafor .com/article/02/10/2025/trust-in-news-summit.

Chapter 1: An Existential Crisis

1 Mindich, D. (2016) 'For journalists covering Trump, a Murrow moment', *Columbia Journalism Review*. Available at: https:// www.cjr.org/analysis/trump_inspires_murrow_moment_for_jo urnalism.php.

2 Rosen, J. (2016) 'Donald Trump is crashing the system. Journalists need to build a new one', *The Washington Post*. Available at: https://www.washingtonpost.com/news/in-theory/wp/2016/07

/13/donald-trump-is-crashing-the-system-journalists-need-to
-build-a-new-one/.

3 Rutenberg, J. (2016) 'Trump is testing the norms of objectivity in
   journalism', *The New York Times*. Available at: https://www.nyt
   imes.com/2016/08/08/business/balance-fairness-and-a-proudly
   -provocative-presidential-candidate.html.

4 Sullivan, M. (2016) 'A call to action for journalists covering
   President Trump', *The Washington Post*. Available at: https://
   www.washingtonpost.com/lifestyle/style/a-call-to-action-for-jo
   urnalists-in-covering-president-trump/2016/11/09/a87d4946
   -a63e-11e6-8042-f4d111c862d1_story.html.

5 Sullivan, M. (2022) 'If Trump runs again, do not cover him
   the same way: A journalist's manifesto', *The Washington Post*.
   Available at: https://www.washingtonpost.com/magazine/2022
   /10/12/margaret-sullivan-how-media-should-cover-trump-next
   -campaign/.

6 Swisher, K. (2017) 'Washington Post's Marty Baron: We're not at
   war with [Trump] administration, we're at work', Code Media.
   Available at: https://www.youtube.com/watch?v=r0frvdLNqTI.

7 Adler, S. (2017) 'Covering Trump the Reuters way', *Reuters*.
   Available at: https://www.reuters.com/article/technology/cover
   ing-trump-the-reuters-way-idUSKBN15F26V/.

8 Spayd, L. (2016) 'The truth about "false balance"', *The New York
   Times*. Available at: https://www.nytimes.com/2016/09/11/pub
   lic-editor/the-truth-about-false-balance.html.

9 Spayd, L. (2016) 'When to call a lie a lie', *The New York Times*.
   Available at: https://www.nytimes.com/2016/09/20/public-edit
   or/trump-birther-lie-liz-spayd-public-editor.html.

10 Métivier, M. (2021) 'Big News: Is media driving political
   polarization?', *CBC News*. Available at: https://www.youtube
   .com/watch?v=AYAbBz6wUpo&t=1595s.

11 Taibbi, M. (2020) 'The American press is destroying itself', *Racket
   News*. Available at: https://www.racket.news/p/the-news-media
   -is-destroying-itself.

12 Henley, T. (2022) 'Transcript: David Greenberg', *Lean Out*

with Tara Henley. Available at: https://tarahenley.substack.com /p/transcript-david-greenberg.

Chapter 2: A Failing Business Model

1 Henley, T. (2023) 'Transcript: Jen Gerson', *Lean Out with Tara Henley*. Available at: https://tarahenley.substack.com/p/transcript-jen-gerson.
2 Farhi, P. (2024) 'Is American journalism headed toward an "extinction-level event"?', *The Atlantic*. Available at: https:// www.theatlantic.com/ideas/archive/2024/01/media-layoffs-la -times/677285/.
3 Reynolds Lewis, K. (2025) 'Coping with media layoffs', *Nieman Reports*. Available at: https://niemanreports.org/resources-layof fs-laid-off-journalists/.
4 Henley, T. (2023) 'Transcript: Peter Menzies', *Lean Out with Tara Henley*. Available at: https://tarahenley.substack.com /p/transcript-peter-menzies.
5 Taibbi, M. (2019) *Hate, Inc.: Why Today's Media Makes Us Despise One Another.* New York: OR Books.
6 Henley, T. (2022) 'Bad news', *Lean Out with Tara Henley*. Available at: https://tarahenley.substack.com/p/bad-news.
7 Metzger, Z. (2024) 'The state of local news', *Local News Initiative*. Available at: https://localnewsinitiative.northwestern.edu/pro jects/state-of-local-news/2024/report/#executive-summary.
8 Fischer, S. (2024) 'Most U.S. counties have little to no local news sources', *Axios*. Available at: https://www.axios.com/2024/10/24 /most-us-counties-have-little-to-no-local-news-sources.
9 Henley, T. (2023) 'Transcript: Sohrab Ahmari', *Lean Out with Tara Henley*. Available at: https://tarahenley.substack.com /p/transcript-sohrab-ahmari.
10 Clegg, E. and Kennedy, D. (2024) *What Works in Community News: Media Startups, News Deserts, and the Future of the Fourth Estate.* Boston, MA: Beacon Press.
11 Henley, T. (2024) 'Transcript: Ellen Clegg and Dan Kennedy',

Lean Out with Tara Henley. Available at: https://tarahenley.sub stack.com/p/transcript-ellen-clegg-and-dan-kennedy.

12 Henley, T. (2023) 'Transcript: Jen Gerson', *Lean Out with Tara Henley.* Available at: https://tarahenley.substack.com/p/transcri pt-jen-gerson.

13 Kovach, B. and Rosenstiel, T. (2021) *The Elements of Journalism: What Newspeople Should Know and the Public Should Expect.* New York: Crown.

14 Henley, T. (2022) 'Transcript: Holly Doan', *Lean Out with Tara Henley.* Available at: https://tarahenley.substack.com/p/transcri pt-holly-doan.

15 Willnat, L. (2022) 'The American journalist under attack', *The American Journalist.* Available at: https://www.theamericanjour nalist.org/_files/ugd/46a507_4fe1c4d6ec6d4c229895282965258 a7a.pdf.

16 Benton, J. (2024) 'Is the New York Times' newsroom just a bunch of ivy leaguers? (Kinda, sorta.)', *Nieman Lab.* Available at: https://www.niemanlab.org/2024/02/is-the-new-york-times-ne wsroom-just-a-bunch-of-ivy-leaguers-kinda-sorta/.

17 Wai, J. and Perina, K. (2018) 'Expertise in journalism: Factors shaping a cognitive and culturally elite profession', *Journal of Expertise*, 1(1): 57–78.

18 Grieco, E. (2019) 'One-in-five U.S. newsroom employees live in New York, Los Angeles or D.C.', *Pew Research Center.* Available at: https://www.pewresearch.org/short-reads/2019/10/24/one-in-five-u-s-newsroom-employees-live-in-new-york-los-angeles -or-d-c/.

19 Krakauer, S. (2023) *Uncovered: How the Media Got Cozy with Power, Abandoned Its Principles, and Lost the People.* New York: Center Street, Hachette Book Group.

20 Henley, T. (2023) 'Transcript: Steve Krakauer', *Lean Out with Tara Henley.* Available at: https://tarahenley.substack.com /p/transcript-steve-krakauer.

21 Henley, T. (2024) 'Transcript: Andy Mills', *Lean Out with Tara*

Henley. Available at: https://tarahenley.substack.com/p/transcript-andy-mills.

22 Bianco, M. (2014) 'This brave woman's horrifying photo has become a viral rallying cry against sexual harassment', *Mic.* Available at: https://www.mic.com/articles/97632/this-brave-woman-s-horrifying-photo-has-become-a-viral-rallying-cry-against-sexual-harassment.

23 Davidson, L. (2014) 'The problematic Disney body image trend we're not talking about', *Mic.* Available at: https://www.mic.com/articles/87331/the-problematic-disney-body-image-trend-we-re-not-talking-about.

24 Grigoriadis, V. (2007) 'Gawker and the rage of the creative underclass', *New York Magazine.* Available at: https://nymag.com/news/features/39319/.

25 Walker, M. (2021) 'U.S. newsroom employment has fallen 26% since 2008', *Pew Research Center.* Available at: https://www.pewresearch.org/short-reads/2021/07/13/u-s-newsroom-employment-has-fallen-26-since-2008/.

26 Jeffries, A. (2017) 'Mic's drop: How Mic.com exploited social justice for clicks, and then abandoned a staff that believed in it', *The Outline.* Available at: https://theoutline.com/post/2156/mic-com-and-the-cynicism-of-modern-media.

Chapter 3: A Great Awokening

1 Burgis, B. (2021) *Canceling Comedians While the World Burns: A Critique of the Contemporary Left.* Winchester, UK: Zero Books.

2 Henley, T. (2022) 'Canceling comedians while the world burns', *Lean Out with Tara Henley.* Available at: https://tarahenley.substack.com/p/canceling-comedians-while-the-world.

3 Henley, T. (2021) 'Writers call for a more nuanced alternative to "cancel culture"', *The Globe and Mail.* Available at: https://www.theglobeandmail.com/arts/books/article-writers-call-for-a-more-nuanced-alternative-to-cancel-culture/.

4 deBoer, F. (2021) 'It's all just displacement', *Freddie deBoer.*

Available at: https://freddiedeboer.substack.com/p/its-all-just
-displacement.

5 Henley, T. (2022) 'Transcript: Freddie deBoer', *Lean Out with
   Tara Henley*. Available at: https://tarahenley.substack.com
   /p/transcript-freddie-deboer.

6 deBoer, F. (2023) *How Elites Ate the Social Justice Movement*.
   New York: Simon & Schuster.

7 Neiman, S. (2023) *Left Is Not Woke*. Cambridge, UK: Polity.

8 Grieco, E. (2020) 'Americans' main sources for political news
   vary by party and age', *Pew Research Center*. Available at:
   https://www.pewresearch.org/short-reads/2020/04/01/
   americans-main-sources-for-political-news-vary-by-party-and-
   age/.

9 Thurman, N. (2025) 'UK journalists in the 2020s: Who they are,
   how they work, and what they think', *Reuters Institute for the
   Study of Journalism*. Available at: https://reutersinstitute.politics
   .ox.ac.uk/sites/default/files/2025-04/uk_journalists_in_the_20
   20s.pdf.

10 Willnat, L. (2022) 'The American journalist under attack', *The
   American Journalist*. Available at: https://www.theamericanjour
   nalist.org/_files/ugd/46a507_4fe1c4d6ec6d4c229895282965258
   a7a.pdf.

11 Berliner, U. (2024) 'I've been at NPR for 25 years. here's how we
   lost America's trust', *The Free Press*. Available at: https://www.th
   efp.com/p/npr-editor-how-npr-lost-americas-trust.

12 Hobolt, S.B., Lawall, K. and Tilley, J. (2024) 'The polarizing effect
   of partisan echo chambers', *American Political Science Review*,
   118(3): 1464–79.

13 Deresiewicz, W. (2022) 'Escaping American tribalism', *UnHerd*.
   Available at: https://unherd.com/2022/03/escaping-american-tr
   ibalism/.

14 Henley, T. (2022) 'Transcript: William Deresiewicz', *Lean Out
   with Tara Henley*. Available at: https://tarahenley.substack.com
   /p/transcript-william-deresiewicz.

15 Honderich, H. (2025) 'CIA says lab leak most likely source of

Covid outbreak', *BBC News*. Available at: https://www.bbc
.com/news/articles/cd9qjjj4zy5o.

16 Clark, C.J., Isch, C., Everett, J.A.C. and Shariff, A.F. (2023) *Even
When Ideologies Align, People Distrust Politicized Institutions*
[Manuscript in preparation]. Available at: https://osf.io/pre
prints/psyarxiv/sfubr_v1.

17 Zhang, F.J. (2023) 'Political endorsement by *Nature* and trust
in scientific expertise during COVID-19', *Nature Human
Behaviour*, 7: 696–706.

18 Henley, T. (2023) 'Transcript: Azim Shariff', *Lean Out with Tara
Henley*. Available at: https://tarahenley.substack.com/p/tran
script-azim-shariff.

19 Rozado, D., Al-Gharbi, M. and Halberstadt, J. (2023) 'Prevalence
of prejudice-denoting words in news media discourse: A chrono-
logical analysis', *Social Science Computer Review*, 41(1): 99–122.

20 Hawkins, S. (2018) 'Hidden tribes: A study of America's polarized
landscape', *More in Common*. Available at: https://hiddentribes
.us/media/qfpekz4g/hidden_tribes_report.pdf.

21 Pew Research Center (2021) 'Beyond red vs. blue: The political
typology', *Pew Research Center*. Available at: https://www.pew
research.org/politics/2021/11/09/progressive-left/.

22 Fuller, T. (2020) 'How one of America's whitest cities became
the center of B.L.M. protests', *The New York Times*. Available at:
https://www.nytimes.com/2020/07/24/us/portland-oregon-pro
tests-white-race.html.

23 Williams, J.C. (2025) *Outclassed: How the Left Lost the Working
Class and How to Win Them Back.* New York: St. Martin's Press,
p. 49.

24 Henley, T. (2025) 'Transcript: Joan C. Williams', *Lean Out with
Tara Henley*. Available at: https://tarahenley.substack.com
/p/transcript-joan-c-williams.

25 Kaufmann, E. (20234) 'The politics of the culture wars in contemporary Canada', *Macdonald-Laurier Institute*. Available at:
https://macdonaldlaurier.ca/politics-of-culture-wars-canada/.

26 Harmon, A. and Tavernise, S. (2020) 'One big difference about

George Floyd protests: Many white faces', *The New York Times*. Available at: https://www.nytimes.com/2020/06/12/us/george-floyd-white-protesters.html.

27 al-Gharbi, M. (2024) *We Have Never Been Woke: The Cultural Contradictions of a New Elite.* Princeton, NJ: Princeton University Press, p. 303.

28 Henley, T. (2024) 'Transcript: Musa al-Gharbi', *Lean Out with Tara Henley*. Available at: https://tarahenley.substack.com /p/transcript-musa-al-gharbi.

29 al-Gharbi, *We Have Never Been Woke*, pp. 8, 48, 83, 84.

30 Cohen, R. (1993) *When the Old Left Was Young: Student Radicals and America's First Mass Student Movement, 1929–1941.* S.l.: Oxford University Press.

31 al-Gharbi, *We Have Never Been Woke*, pp. 84, 85, 88, 93.

32 Turchin, P. (2023) *End Times: Elites, Counter-Elites and the Path of Political Disintegration.* London: Penguin Books.

33 Henley, T. (2024) 'Transcript: Musa al-Gharbi', *Lean Out with Tara Henley*. Available at: https://tarahenley.substack.com /p/transcript-musa-al-gharbi.

34 al-Gharbi, *We Have Never Been Woke*, p. 70.

35 Rosenstiel, T. (2021) 'A new way of looking at trust in media: Do Americans share journalism's core values?', *National Opinion Research Center*. Available at: https://www.norc.org/content /dam/norc-org/documents/standard-projects-pdf/A-New-Way -of-Looking-at-Trust-in-Media-1.pdf.

36 Forman-Katz, N. (2022) 'U.S. journalists differ from the public in their views of "bothsidesism" in journalism', *Pew Research Center*. Available at: https://www.pewresearch.org/short-reads /2022/07/13/u-s-journalists-differ-from-the-public-in-their-views-of-bothsidesism-in-journalism/.

37 Ripley, A. (2021) *High Conflict: Why We Get Trapped and How We Get Out.* New York: Simon & Schuster.

38 Henley, T. (2022) 'Get insanely curious when no one else is curious', *Lean Out with Tara Henley*. Available at: https://tara henley.substack.com/p/get-insanely-curious-when-no-one.

39 Lukianoff, G. and Schlott, R. (2023) *The Canceling of the American Mind: How Cancel Culture Undermines Trust, Destroys Institutions, and Threatens Us All.* New York: Simon & Schuster.

40 Henley, T. (2023) 'Transcript: Greg Lukianoff', *Lean Out with Tara Henley.* Available at: https://tarahenley.substack.com /p/transcript-greg-lukianoff.

41 Henley, T. (2024) 'Transcript: Nellie Bowles', *Lean Out with Tara Henley.* Available at: https://tarahenley.substack.com/p/transcript-nellie-bowles.

42 Bowles, N. (2024) *Morning After the Revolution: Dispatches from the Wrong Side of History.* New York: Thesis, pp. xvii, xxv.

43 Schwartz, I. (2020) Seattle mayor Durkan: Chaz has a "Block party atmosphere," could turn into "Summer of love"', *Real Clear Politics.* Available at: https://www.realclearpolitics.com/video /2020/06/12/seattle_mayor_durkan_chaz_has_a_block_party_at mosphere_could_turn_into_summer_of_love.html.

44 Golden, H. (2020) 'Seattle protesters take over city blocks to create police-free "autonomous zone"', *The Guardian.* Available at: https://www.theguardian.com/us-news/2020/jun/11/chaz-seattle-autonomous-zone-police-protest.

45 Weinberger, H. (2020) 'In Seattle's Chaz, a community garden takes root', *PBS.* Available at: https://www.cascadepbs.org /environment/2020/06/seattles-chaz-community-garden-takes -root/.

46 Bowles, N. (2020) 'Abolish the police? those who survived the chaos in Seattle aren't so sure', *The New York Times.* Available at: https://www.nytimes.com/2020/08/07/us/defund-police-seat tle-protests.html.

47 Cotton, T. (2020) 'Opinion: Send in the troops', *The New York Times.* Available at: https://www.nytimes.com/2020/06/03/ opinion/tom-cotton-protests-military.html.

48 Wulfsohn, J.A. and Fox News (2024) 'Ex-New York Times journalist recalls being "disgusted" by newsroom cancel culture, says the paper allowed it', *Fox News.* Available at: https://www

.foxnews.com/media/ex-new-york-times-journalist-reports-disgusted-newsroom-cancel-culture.

Chapter 4: A Leadership Vacuum

1 Henley, T. (2024) 'Transcript: Michael Powell', *Lean Out with Tara Henley*. Available at: https://tarahenley.substack.com/p/transcript-michael-powell.

2 Cotton, T. (2020) 'Opinion: Send in the troops', *The New York Times*. Available at: https://www.nytimes.com/2020/06/03/opinion/tom-cotton-protests-military.html.

3 Ivie, D. (2020) '*New York Times*' Opinion Editor resigns after Tom Cotton controversy', *Vulture*. Available at: https://www.vulture.com/2020/06/new-york-times-opinion-editor-resigns-after-tom-cotton-op-ed.html.

4 (2020) 'Letter in response to the NYT Opinion Article – Tom Cotton: Send in the troops'. Available at: https://int.nyt.com/data/documenthelper/7004-times-letter/efc475797987966bdaab/optimized/full.pdf.

5 Henley, T. (2024) 'Transcript: Michael Powell', *Lean Out with Tara Henley*. Available at: https://tarahenley.substack.com/p/transcript-michael-powell.

6 Rubenstein, A. (2024) 'I was a heretic at *The New York Times*', *The Atlantic*. Available at: https://www.theatlantic.com/ideas/archive/2024/02/tom-cotton-new-york-times/677546.

7 Wemple, E. (2022) 'Opinion: James Bennet was right', *Washington Post*. https://www.washingtonpost.com/opinions/2022/10/27/new-york-times-tom-cotton-oped-james-bennet/.

8 Weiss, B. (2020) 'Bari Weiss on why she left the *New York Times*', *New York Post*. Available at: https://nypost.com/2020/07/14/bari-weiss-on-why-she-left-the-new-york-times/.

9 Henley, T. (2021) 'How the subscription newsletter service Substack is changing the writing game', *The Globe and Mail*. Available at: https://www.theglobeandmail.com/arts/books/article-how-the-subscription-newsletter-service-substack-is-changing-the/.

10 Fang, L. (2020) '@lhfang', *X* (formerly *Twitter*). Available at: https://x.com/lhfang/status/1268390704645943297.

11 Taibbi, M. (2020) 'The American press is destroying itself', *Racket News*. Available at: https://www.racket.news/p/the-news-media -is-destroying-itself.

12 Henley, T. (2024) 'Transcript: Andy Mills', *Lean Out with Tara Henley*. Available at: https://tarahenley.substack.com/p/transcri pt-andy-mills.

13 Blocked and Reported (2024) 'Episode 201: Mills spills (with Andy Mills)', *Blocked and Reported*. Available at: https://www. blockedandreported.org/p/episode-201-mills-spills-with-andy.

14 Mills, A. (2021) 'Resignation', *Andy Mills*. Available at: https:// www.andymills.work/resignation.

15 Kachka, B. (2018) 'At WNYC, an uncertain path out of scandal', *The Cut (originally published in New York)*. Available at: https:// www.thecut.com/2018/02/at-wnyc-an-uncertain-path-out-of- scandal.html.

16 Cecco, L. (2021) 'Canada drops charges against man who claimed to be IS executioner', *The Guardian*. Available at: https://www.th eguardian.com/world/2021/oct/11/canada-drops-charges-man -lied-about-being-is-executioner-shehroze-chaudhry-terrorism -hoax-laws.

17 Boll, M. and Mills, A. (2024) 'Why doesn't anyone trust the media?', *Reflector*. Available at: https://podcasts.apple.com/ca /podcast/reflector/id1743666262?i=1000677760945.

18 Smith, B. (2021) 'Postcard from Peru: Why the morality plays inside the Times won't stop', *The New York Times*. Available at: https://www.nytimes.com/2021/02/14/business/media/new-yo rk-times-donald-mcneil.html.

19 Tani, M. and Cartwright, L. (2021) 'Star *NY Times* reporter accused of using "n-word," making other racist comments', *The Daily Beast*. Available at: https://www.thedailybeast.com /star-new-york-times-reporter-donald-mcneil-accused-of-using-n- word-making-other-racist-comments/.

20 Tani, M. and Cartwright, L. (2021) '*NY Times* staffers send

"outraged" letter to bosses demanding reporter apologize for racial slur', *The Daily Beast*. Available at: https://www.thedaily beast.com/new-york-times-staffers-sent-outraged-letter-to-bos ses-probe-of-donald-mcneils-racial-slur/.

21 Ismail, A. (2021) 'An exhausting week at the New York Times: Nikole Hannah-Jones on Donald McNeil's resignation, what the reporting got wrong, and how she was involved', *Slate Magazine*. Available at: https://slate.com/news-and-politics/2021 /02/nikole-hannah-jones-don-mcneil-new-york-times-inte rview.html.

22 McNeil Jr, D.G. (2021) 'NYTimes Peru N-word, Part One: Introduction', *Medium*. Available at: https://donaldgmcneiljr19 54.medium.com/nytimes-peru-n-word-part-one-introduction -57eb6a3e0d95.

23 PEN America (2021) 'PEN America responds to resignation of New York Times reporter McNeil', *PEN America*. Available at: https://pen.org/press-release/pen-america-responds-to-resig nation-of-new-york-times-reporter-mcneil/.

24 Stephens, B. (2021) 'Read the column The New York Times didn't want you to see', *New York Post*. Available at: https://nypo st.com/2021/02/11/read-the-column-the-new-york-times-didnt -want-you-read/.

25 Henley, T. (2024) 'Transcript: Andy Mills', *Lean Out with Tara Henley*. Available at: https://tarahenley.substack.com/p/transcri pt-andy-mills.

26 Williams, T.C. (2025) *Summer of Our Discontent: The Age of Certainty and the Demise of Discourse*. New York: Alfred A. Knopf.

27 Henley, T. (2025) 'Transcript: Thomas Chatterton Williams', *Lean Out with Tara Henley*. Available at: https://tarahenley.sub stack.com/p/transcript-thomas-chatterton-williams.

28 Frommer, D. (2020) 'What Alison Roman wants', *The New Consumer*. Available at: https://newconsumer.com/2020/05/ali son-roman-interview/.

29 Bradley, L. (2020) 'Alison Roman bashed Marie Kondo and

Chrissy Teigen, and it did not spark joy', *The Daily Beast*. Available at: https://www.thedailybeast.com/alison-roman-bashed-marie-kondo-and-chrissy-teigen-and-it-did-not-spark-joy/.

30 Henley, T. (2023) 'Transcript: Meghan Daum', *Lean Out with Tara Henley*. Available at: https://tarahenley.substack.com/p/transcript-meghan-daum-89e.

31 Collins, L. (2021) 'Alison Roman just can't help herself', *The New Yorker*. Available at: https://www.newyorker.com/magazine/2021/12/20/alison-roman-just-cant-help-herself.

32 Mesley, W. (2021) 'Opinion: I made mistakes. But my departure wasn't the solution to the CBC's problem with racism', *The Globe and Mail*. Available at: https://www.theglobeandmail.com/opinion/article-the-cbcs-issues-with-systemic-racism-go-beyond-the-two-worst-moments/.

33 The Sound Off Podcast (2022) 'Wendy Mesley: Freedom 65', *The Sound Off Podcast*. Available at: https://www.youtube.com/watch?v=0XEISWPZ1co.

34 Jivani, J. (2022) 'Bell finally admits why they fired me.', *Jamil Jivani*. Available at: https://jamiljivani.substack.com/p/bell-admits-truth.

35 Humphreys, A. (2022) 'Bell's defence for firing only Black radio host says he showed disdain for diversity initiatives', *The National Post*. Available at: https://nationalpost.com/news/bells-firing-only-black-radio-host.

36 Henley, T. (2022) 'Diversity of thought', *Lean Out with Tara Henley*. Available at: https://tarahenley.substack.com/p/diversity-of-thought.

37 Henley, T. (2023) 'Transcript: Michael Lind', *Lean Out with Tara Henley*. Available at: https://tarahenley.substack.com/p/transcript-michael-lind.

38 Bennet, J. (2023) '1843: When the New York Times lost its way', *The Economist*. Available at: https://www.economist.com/1843/2023/12/14/when-the-new-york-times-lost-its-way.

Chapter 5: A Rejection of Objectivity

1 Smith, B. (2020) 'Inside the revolts erupting in America's big newsrooms', *The New York Times*. Available at: https://www.nytimes.com/2020/06/07/business/media/new-york-times-washington-post-protests.html.

2 The Washington Post (2014) 'Post's Lowery detained in Ferguson', *The Washington Post*. Available at: https://www.washingtonpost.com/video/national/post-reporter-detained-in-ferguson/2014/08/13/b0fc5720-2354-11e4-8b10-7db129976abb_video.html.

3 New Day (2014) 'Two reporters arrested overnight in Ferguson, Missouri; interview with Wesley Lowery and Ryan Reilly', *CNN*. Available at: https://transcripts.cnn.com/show/nday/date/2014-08-14/segment/06.

4 Baron, M. (2023) *Collision of Power: Trump, Bezos, and the Washington Post*. New York: Flatiron Books, 366–72.

5 Chan, J.C. (2020) 'Wesley Lowery suggests his Washington Post editors "threatened" him over his tweets', *TheWrap*. Available at: https://www.thewrap.com/wesley-lowery-suggests-his-washington-post-editors-threatened-him-over-his-tweets/.

6 Lowery, W. (2020) 'Opinion: A reckoning over objectivity, led by black journalists', *The New York Times*. Available at: https://www.nytimes.com/2020/06/23/opinion/objectivity-black-journalists-coronavirus.html.

7 Gessen, M. (2020) 'Why are some journalists afraid of "moral clarity"?', *The New Yorker*. Available at: https://www.newyorker.com/news/our-columnists/why-are-some-journalists-afraid-of-moral-clarity.

8 Wallace, L.R. (2019) *The View from Somewhere: Undoing the Myth of Journalistic Objectivity*. Chicago: The University of Chicago Press.

9 Mattar, P. (2020) 'Objectivity is a privilege afforded to white journalists', *The Walrus*. Available at: https://thewalrus.ca/objectivity-is-a-privilege-afforded-to-white-journalists/.

10 Callison, C. and Young, M.L. (2019) *Reckoning: Journalism's Limits and Possibilities*. New York: Oxford University Press.

11 Greenberg, D. (2022) 'The war on objectivity in American journalism', *Liberties*. Available at: https://libertiesjournal.com /articles/the-war-on-objectivity-in-american-journalism/.

12 Henley, T. (2022) 'Transcript: David Greenberg', *Lean Out with Tara Henley*. Available at: https://tarahenley.substack.com /p/transcript-david-greenberg.

13 Henley, T. (2023) 'Transcript: George Packer', *Lean Out with Tara Henley*. Available at: https://tarahenley.substack.com /p/transcript-george-packer.

14 Downie, L. (2023) 'Newsrooms that move beyond "objectivity" can build trust', *The Washington Post*. Available at: https://www .washingtonpost.com/opinions/2023/01/30/newsrooms-news-reporting-objectivity-diversity/.

15 Schudson, M. (1978) *Discovering the News: A Social History of American Newspapers*. United States: Basic Books, p. 157.

16 Schudson, *Discovering the News*, pp. 28, 21.

17 Schudson, *Discovering the News*, pp. 106, 120, 142.

18 Lippmann, W. (2020) *Liberty and the News*. Princeton, NJ: Princeton University Press.

19 Lippmann, W. (2022) *Public Opinion*. Blacksburg, VA: Warbler Classics.

20 Schudson, *Discovering the News*, pp. 160, 161.

21 Darcy, O. (2023) 'Christiane Amanpour reflects on her 40 years at CNN and explains why her "be truthful, not neutral" mantra is more vital than ever', *CNN*. Available at: https://edition.cnn.com /2023/09/13/media/christiane-amanpour-cnn-reliable-sources.

22 Cunningham, B. (2003) 'Re-thinking objectivity', *Columbia Journalism Review*. Available at: https://www.cjr.org/feature/ret hinking_objectivity.php.

23 Greenhouse, L. (2017) *Just a Journalist: On the Press, Life, and the Spaces Between*. Cambridge, MA: Harvard University Press, p. xii.

24 Kovach, B. and Rosenstiel, T. (2021) *The Elements of Journalism: What Newspeople Should Know and the Public Should Expect.* New York: Crown, p. xxviii.

25 Sulzberger, A.G. (2023) 'Journalism's essential value', *Columbia Journalism Review.* Available at: https://www.cjr.org/special_report/ag-sulzberger-new-york-times-journalisms-essential-value-objectivity-independence.php.

26 Kovach and Rosenstiel, *The Elements of Journalism*, p. xxi.

27 Sullivan, M. (2022) *Newsroom Confidential: Lessons (and Worries) from an Ink-Stained Life.* New York: St. Martin's Press, p. 200.

28 Baron, M. (2023) 'We want objective judges and doctors. Why not journalists too?', *The Washington Post.* Available at: https://www.washingtonpost.com/opinions/2023/03/24/journalism-objectivity-trump-misinformation-marty-baron/.

29 Newman, N. (2021) 'The relevance of impartial news in a polarised world', *Reuters Institute for the Study of Journalism.* Available at: https://reutersinstitute.politics.ox.ac.uk/sites/default/files/2021-10/Vir_the_relevance_of_impartial_news_in_a_polarised_world_FINAL_0.pdf.

30 Schwalbe, M.C., Joseff, K., Woolley, S. and Cohen, G.L. (2024) 'When politics trumps truth: Political concordance versus veracity as a determinant of believing, sharing, and recalling the news', *Journal of Experimental Psychology: General*, 153(10): 2524–51.

31 Underwood, P.L. (2024) 'News consumers are more influenced by political alignment than by truth, new study shows', *Stanford Report.* Available at: https://news.stanford.edu/stories/2024/10/new-study-shows-that-partisanship-trumps-truth.

32 Schudson, M. (2022) 'What does "trust in the media" mean?', *Daedalus*, 151(4): 144–60.

Chapter 6: A Failure to Acknowledge Mistakes

1 The Munk Debates (2022) 'Munk Debate Podcast: Mainstream Media Debate', *YouTube.* Available at: https://www.youtube.com/watch?v=3vkgROIINEs.

2 Cayley, D. (2020) 'The Prognosis: Looking the consequences in the eye', *Literary Review of Canada*. Available at: https://reviewcanada.ca/magazine/2020/10/the-prognosis/.

3 Kazemi, P., Les, J.E. and Fulford, M. (2022) 'Opinion: Beware misinformation about COVID risks to kids', *The National Post*. Available at: https://nationalpost.com/opinion/opinion-beware-misinformation-about-covid-risks-to-kids.

4 Cayley, D. (2020) 'The prognosis.

5 Nocera, J. and McLean, B. (2023) 'COVID lockdowns were a giant experiment. It was a failure', *New York Intelligencer*. Available at: https://nymag.com/intelligencer/article/covid-lockdowns-big-fail-joe-nocera-bethany-mclean-book-excerpt.html.

6 Henley, T. (2023) 'Transcript: Joe Nocera', *Lean Out with Tara Henley*. Available at: https://tarahenley.substack.com/p/transcript-joe-nocera.

7 Nocera, J. and McLean, B. (2023) *The Big Fail: What the Pandemic Revealed About Who America Protects and Who It Leaves Behind.* New York: Portfolio/Penguin.

8 Henley, T. (2023) 'Transcript: Mark Woolhouse', *Lean Out with Tara Henley*. Available at: https://tarahenley.substack.com/p/transcript-mark-woolhouse.

9 Henley, T. (2025) 'Transcript: Stephen Macedo & Frances Lee', *Lean Out with Tara Henley*. Available at: https://tarahenley.substack.com/p/transcript-stephen-macedo-and-frances.

10 MacGillis, A. (2020) 'The students left behind by remote learning', *ProPublica*. Available at: https://www.propublica.org/article/the-students-left-behind-by-remote-learning.

11 Mervosh, S., Miller, C.C. and Paris, F. (2024) 'What the data says about pandemic school closures, four years later', *The New York Times*. Available at: https://www.nytimes.com/2024/03/18/upshot/pandemic-school-closures-data.html.

12 Zweig, D. (2025) *An Abundance of Caution: American Schools, the Virus, and a Story of Bad Decisions.* Cambridge, MA: The MIT Press.

13 Henley, T. (2025) 'Transcript: David Zweig', *Lean Out with Tara*

Henley. Available at: https://tarahenley.substack.com/p/tran script-david-zweig.

14 MacGillis, A. (2024) 'Has school become optional?', *The New Yorker.* Available at: https://www.newyorker.com/magazine/20 24/01/15/has-school-become-optional.

15 Henley, T. (2024) 'Transcript: Alec MacGillis', *Lean Out with Tara Henley.* Available at: https://tarahenley.substack.com /p/transcript-alec-macgillis.

16 Kamenetz, A. (2022) *The Stolen Year: How COVID Changed Children's Lives, and Where We Go Now.* New York: PublicAffairs.

17 Henley, T. (2022) 'The stolen year', *Lean Out with Tara Henley.* Available at: https://tarahenley.substack.com/p/the-stolen-year.

18 Mason, G. (2022) 'Opinion: Trucker convoy has evolved into something far more dangerous', *The Globe and Mail.* Available at: https://www.theglobeandmail.com/opinion/article-trucker-convoy-has-evolved-into-something-far-more-dangerous/.

19 Arthur, B. (2022) '@bruce_arthur', *X* (formerly *Twitter*). Available at: https://x.com/bruce_arthur/status/1490196230139523075.

20 van Oldenbarneveld, L. (2022) '@LucyvanOlden', *X* (formerly *Twitter*). Available at: https://x.com/LucyvanOlden/status/1488 670509588008961.

21 Public Order Emergency Commission (POEC) (2023) 'Report of the public inquiry into the 2022 public order emergency: Final report', *Public Order Emergency Commission.* Available at: https://publicorderemergencycommission.ca/final-report/.

22 Reuters (2024) 'Trudeau govt to appeal ruling on use of emergency powers to end 2022 protests', *Reuters.* Available at: https://www .reuters.com/world/americas/ottawa-appeal-ruling-canadas-use -emergency-powers-was-unreasonable-2024-01-23/.

23 Thompson, E. (2022) 'Convoy money didn't come from 'foreign actors', CSIS told officials during protest.' *CBC News.* Available at: https://www.cbc.ca/news/politics/convoy-protest-money-cs is-1.6621944.

24 The Editorial Board (2025) 'The Crown Versus the Truckers', *The Wall Street Journal.* Available at: https://www.wsj.com/opin

ion/canada-freedom-convoy-truckers-protests-vaccines-tamara
-lich-chris-barber-prosecutions-584187d8.

25 Henley, T. (2024) 'Transcript: Ryan Alford', *Lean Out with Tara Henley*. Available at: https://tarahenley.substack.com/p/transcript-ryan-alford.

26 Osman, L. (2022) 'Calling Ottawa protests "peaceful" downplays non-violent dangers, critics say', *The Canadian Press/CTV News*. Available at: https://www.ctvnews.ca/canada/article/calling-ottawa-protests-peaceful-downplays-non-violent-dangers-critics-say/.

27 Fraser, D. (2023) 'Protesters urinated, defecated on church property, convoy trial hears', *CBC News*. Available at: https://www.cbc.ca/news/canada/ottawa/protesters-urinated-defecated-on-church-property-convoy-trial-hears-1.6993786.

28 Henley, T. (2025) 'Transcript: David Cayley', *Lean Out with Tara Henley*. Available at: https://tarahenley.substack.com/p/transcript-david-cayley.

29 The Fifth Estate (2022) 'The convoy and the questions: How a protest paralyzed a capital', *CBC News*. Available at: https://www.cbc.ca/player/play/video/1.6363835.

30 Henley, T. (2022) 'Meet the press', *Lean Out with Tara Henley*. Available at: https://tarahenley.substack.com/p/meet-the-press.

31 Subramanya, R. (2022) 'What the truckers want', *The Free Press*. Available at: https://www.thefp.com/p/what-the-truckers-want.

32 National Post Staff (2022) 'Liberal MP Joël Lightbound's full remarks: "it's time to choose positive, not coercive methods"', *The National Post*. Available at: https://nationalpost.com/news/politics/joel-lightbound-full-transcript.

Chapter 7: A Failure to Insulate the Media from Power

1 Henley, T. (2025) 'Transcript: David Zweig', *Lean Out with Tara Henley*. Available at: https://tarahenley.substack.com/p/transcript-david-zweig.

2 PBS NewsHour (2024) 'Brooks and Capehart on voters' concerns

about Biden's age, Trump's ballot eligibility', *PBS News*. Available at: https://www.youtube.com/watch?v=rJEmS1F_tV8.

3 Glueck, K., Hsu, T. and Li, A. (2024) 'How misleading videos are trailing Biden as he battles age doubts', *The New York Times*. Available at: https://www.nytimes.com/2024/06/21/us/politics/biden-age-videos.html.

4 Linskey, A. and Hughes, S. (2024) 'Behind closed doors, Biden shows signs of slipping', *The Wall Street Journal*. Available at: https://www.wsj.com/politics/policy/joe-biden-age-election-2024-8ee15246.

5 Jones, T. (2024) 'The Wall Street Journal's story on Biden's mental fitness: Fair or foul?', *Poynter*. Available at: https://www.poynter.org/commentary/2024/wall-street-journal-biden-mental-sharpness/.

6 Wulfsohn, J.A. (2025) 'Credibility crisis: Wall Street Journal Report on Biden "slipping" was smeared by media', *Fox News*. Available at: https://www.foxnews.com/media/credibility-crisis-wall-street-journals-report-biden-showing-signs-slipping-smeared-liberal-media.

7 Rubin, J. (2024) 'For presidents, it's not age but judgment that matters', *The Washington Post*. Available at: https://www.washingtonpost.com/opinions/2024/06/09/wall-street-journal-biden-slipping-article/.

8 Darcy, O. (2024) 'The Wall Street Journal's story about Biden's mental acuity suffers from glaring problems', *CNN*. Available at: https://www.cnn.com/2024/06/06/media/wall-street-journal-biden-mental-acuity/index.html.

9 Tani, M. (2024) 'Top liberal media voices turn on Biden', *Semafor*. Available at: https://www.semafor.com/article/06/27/2024/top-liberal-media-voices-turn-on-biden.

10 Nuzzi, O. (2024) 'The conspiracy of silence to protect Joe Biden', *New York Intelligencer*. Available at: https://nymag.com/intelligencer/article/conspiracy-of-silence-to-protect-joe-biden.html.

11 Tapper, J. and Thompson, A. (2025) *Original Sin: President*

Biden's Decline, Its Cover-Up, and His Disastrous Choice to Run Again. New York: Penguin Press.

12 The Megyn Kelly Show (2025) '"Original Sin" authors address "gaslighting," critiques, and reaction from the left and right', *YouTube.* Available at: https://www.youtube.com/watch?v=WD6Vb_vLphE.

13 Washington Week (2025) 'When Biden started showing signs of decline', *YouTube.* Available at: https://www.youtube.com/watch?v=mn_Gq6ASVMQ.

14 Blacklock's Reporter (2024) 'How subsidies failed', *Blacklock's Reporter.* Available at: https://www.blacklocks.ca/guest_commentary/our-submission-to-the-commons-heritage-committee/.

15 Hoffman, J. (2024) 'SaltWire network files for creditor protection, has $94M in debt', *CBC News.* Available at: https://www.cbc.ca/news/canada/nova-scotia/saltwire-creditor-protection-newspaers-atlantic-canada-nova-scotia-1.7140521.

16 Blacklock's Reporter (2024) 'Public opposes media bailout', *Blacklock's Reporter.* Available at: https://www.blacklocks.ca/public-opposes-media-bailout/.

17 Unifor (2024) 'Lana Payne speaks at the HoC Canadian Heritage Standing Committee on state of Canadian media landscape', *Unifor.* Available at: https://www.unifor.org/news/all-news/lana-payne-speaks-hoc-canadian-heritage-standing-committee-state-canadian-media.

18 Henley, T. (2023) 'Weekend reads: Breaking the news', *Lean Out with Tara Henley.* Available at: https://tarahenley.substack.com/p/weekend-reads-breaking-the-news.

19 Henley, T. (2023) 'Weekend reads: The postmedia effect', *Lean Out with Tara Henley.* Available at: https://tarahenley.substack.com/p/weekend-reads-the-postmedia-effect.

20 Korzinski, D. (2023) 'As newsrooms grapple with shifting media landscape, most Canadians oppose government intervention', *Angus Reid Institute.* Available at: https://angusreid.org/canada

-media-consolidation-torstar-postmedia-government-funding
-cbc/.

Chapter 8: A Fork in the Road

1 On the Media (2021) 'How it started, how it's going', *WNYC Studios*. Available at: https://www.wnycstudios.org/podcasts/otm /episodes/on-the-media-how-it-started-how-its-going.

2 Garfield, B. (2022) 'Some personal news', *Bully Pulpit*. Available at: https://bullypulpit.substack.com/p/some-personal-news.

3 On the Media (2023) 'What a year', *WNYC Studios*. Available at: https://www.wnycstudios.org/podcasts/otm/episodes/on-the -media-what-a-year.

4 SBU Journalism (2024) 'The unique challenges of reporting on the 2024 election', *YouTube*. Available at: https://www.youtube.com /watch?v=GHudwxJ68xw.

5 Smith, B. (2024) 'Joe Kahn: "the Newsroom is not a safe space"', *Semafor*. Available at: https://www.semafor.com/article/05/05/20 24/joe-kahn-the-newsroom-is-not-a-safe-space.

6 Pfeiffer, D. (2024) 'Why Biden won't do a New York Times interview', *The Message Box*. Available at: https://www.message boxnews.com/p/why-biden-wont-do-a-new-york-times.

Chapter 9: The Future of News

1 Solnit, R. (2024) 'Our mistake was to think we lived in a better country than we do', *The Guardian*. Available at: https://www .theguardian.com/commentisfree/2024/nov/07/us-progressive -election-trump-maga.

2 Robertson, K. (2025) 'Trump and Musk attack journalists by name in social media posts', *The New York Times*. Available at: https://www.nytimes.com/2025/02/07/business/media/trump -musk-attack-journalists.html.

3 Hudson, J. and Barr, J. (2025) 'State Dept. orders cancellation of news subscriptions around the world', *The Washington Post*. Available at: https://www.washingtonpost.com/style/media/20

25/02/18/state-department-news-subscriptions-trump-media
-crackdown/.

4   Stelter, B. (2025) 'The White House bans the AP indefinitely over
the use of "Gulf of Mexico"', *CNN*. Available at: https://www
.cnn.com/2025/02/14/media/white-house-ap-ban-air-force-one
-oval-office-gulf-of-mexico.

5   Bauder, D. (2025) 'AP wins reinstatement to White House events
after judge rules government can't bar its journalists', *AP News*.
Available at: https://apnews.com/article/trump-ap-media-court
-white-house-events-access-f346a0efe87c1dec4d6f90e6041a
bd09).

6   Scribner, H. (2025) 'Pentagon to move NBC, Politico, NPR and
NYT out of dedicated media offices', *The Washington Post*.
Available at: https://www.washingtonpost.com/style/media/20
25/02/01/pentagon-news-office-politico-new-york-times/.

7   Bensinger, K. (2025) 'Pentagon expands its restrictions on
reporter access', *The New York Times*. Available at: https://www
.nytimes.com/2025/09/20/business/media/pentagon-restric
tions-reporters-hegseth-trump.html.

8   Axelrod, T. (2025) 'Trump's MAGA-friendly press corps', *Axios*.
Available at: https://www.axios.com/2025/04/17/trump-maga-fr
iendly-white-house-press-corps.

9   RSF (2025) 'One month of Trump: Press freedom under siege',
RSF. Available at: https://rsf.org/en/one-month-trump-press-
freedom-under-siege.

10 Dreher, R. (2025) 'Rod Dreher: The radical right is coming for
your sons', *The Free Press*. Available at: https://www.thefp.com
/p/rod-dreher-the-woke-right-is-coming.

11 The Free Press (2025) 'The radical right is coming for your sons
| Bari Weiss & Rod Dreher', *YouTube*. Available at: https://www
.youtube.com/watch?v=GxQ3QqAQ3Uw&t=255s.

12 Doyle, A. (2025) *The End of Woke: How the Culture War Went
Too Far and What to Expect from the Counter-Revolution*.
London: Constable.

13 Henley, T. (2025) 'Transcript: Andrew Doyle', *Lean Out with Tara Henley*. Available at: https://tarahenley.substack.com /p/transcript-andrew-doyle-c69.

14 Henley, T. (2025) 'Transcript: Victor Febres', *Lean Out with Tara Henley*. Available at: https://tarahenley.substack.com/p/tran script-victor-febres.

15 Crane, E. (2025) 'CNN journalist mocked for saying she's "afraid" to travel to the US: "as if I was going to North Korea"', *New York Post*. Available at: https://nypost.com/2025/06/06/us-news/cn ns-christiane-amanpour-mocked-for-being-afraid-to-travel-to -the-us/.

16 Stanley, J., Snyder, T. and Shore, M. (2025) 'We study fascism, and we're leaving the U.S.', *The New York Times*. Available at: https://www.nytimes.com/2025/05/14/opinion/ yale-canada-fascism.html.

17 Snyder, T. (2025) 'Snyder: On leaving Yale', *Yale Daily News*. Available at: https://yaledailynews.com/blog/2025/04/04/snyder -on-leaving-yale/.

18 What a Day Podcast (2025) 'Why One Yale professor chose to leave the U.S.', *Crooked Media*. Available at: https://crooked.com /podcast/why-one-yale-professor-chose-to-leave-the-u-s/.

19 Chan, S. (2025) '@sewellchan'. Available at: https://x.com/sewel lchan/status/1913315814863786061.

20 Sulzberger, A.G. (2025) 'A.G. Sulzberger: A free people need a free press', *The New York Times*. Available at: https://www.ny times.com/2025/05/13/opinion/ag-sulzberger-free-press.html.

21 Pethő, A. (2022) 'I witnessed Orbán crack down on Hungary's free press. Here's my advice to journalists facing similar threats', *Nieman Reports*. Available at: https://niemanreports.org/orban -hungary-free-press-crackdown/.

22 Grynbaum, M.M. (2025) 'ABC suspends Terry Moran for calling Stephen Miller a "world-class hater"', *The New York Times*. Available at: https://www.nytimes.com/2025/06/08/business /media/abc-news-terry-moran-suspended.html.

23 Ripley, A. (2018) 'Complicating the narratives', *Solutions Journalism*. Available at: https://thewholestory.solutionsjournalism.org/complicating-the-narratives-b91ea06ddf63.

24 Henley, T. (2024) 'Transcript: Ross Barkan', *Lean Out with Tara Henley*. Available at: https://tarahenley.substack.com/p/transcript-ross-barkan.

25 Henley, T. (2024) 'Transcript: Ruby Cramer', *Lean Out with Tara Henley*. Available at: https://tarahenley.substack.com/p/transcript-ruby-cramer.

26 Henley, T. (2024) 'Transcript: Alec MacGillis', *Lean Out with Tara Henley*. Available at: https://tarahenley.substack.com/p/transcript-alec-macgillis-8af.

27 Henley, T. (2025) 'Transcript: Vicky Nguyen', *Lean Out with Tara Henley*. Available at: https://tarahenley.substack.com/p/transcript-vicky-nguyen.

Afterword

1 Carter, G. (2025) *When the Going Was Good: An Editor's Adventures During the Last Golden Age of Magazines.* New York: Penguin Press.